Full-Stack JavaScript with TypeScript

Create Robust Apps Using Node, React, Express, and Strong Types

Booker Blunt

Rafael Sanders

Miguel Farmer

Boozman Richard

How to Scan a Barcode to Get a Repository

1. **Install a QR/Barcode Scanner** – Ensure you have a barcode or QR code scanner app installed on your smartphone or use a built-in scanner in **GitHub, GitLab, or Bitbucket.**

2. **Open the Scanner** – Launch the scanner app and grant necessary camera permissions.

3. **Scan the Barcode** – Align the barcode within the scanning frame. The scanner will automatically detect and process it.

4. **Follow the Link** – The scanned result will display a **URL to the repository.** Tap the link to open it in your web browser or Git client.

5. **Clone the Repository** – Use **Git clone** with the provided URL to download the repository to your local machine.

Chapter 1: Introduction to Full-Stack JavaScript Development

Overview of Full-Stack Development

What is Full-Stack Development?

At its core, full-stack development refers to the process of developing both the front-end and back-end parts of an application. Full-stack developers have the ability to work on everything—from what the users interact with (front-end) to the server-side logic and database (back-end). This allows a developer to design and implement all parts of an app, providing them with a complete view of how a product is built and functions.

A full-stack web application is essentially a combination of different layers of technologies that work together to deliver a seamless experience for the end user. These layers include:

1. **Front-End**: This is the part of the application that users interact with directly. It's the visual layout and interface. Think of it as the design, buttons, text, and images you see on a website.

2. **Back-End**: The back-end is the part of the application that processes data, performs logic, and interacts with the database. It handles the "behind-the-scenes" tasks like user authentication, data storage, and business logic.

3. **Database**: Databases store the data that is used by the application. This can range from user details, product listings, and order information. A robust database is key to storing and retrieving data quickly and efficiently.

Why Full-Stack Development Matters

Full-stack development is crucial because it enables flexibility and the ability to quickly iterate on projects. A full-stack developer can build an entire web application from scratch, which reduces dependencies on other team members for different parts of the development process. This approach increases efficiency and helps avoid bottlenecks. Full-stack developers also have a broader understanding of how different parts of an application interact with each other, making them valuable assets in the development process.

Full-stack development is not just for large projects. In fact, it is incredibly useful for startups and smaller teams where resources may be limited. With a full-stack developer, a single person can build an entire working application, from the front end to the back end, without having to rely heavily on specialists in each area.

The Roles of Front-End, Back-End, and Databases in Full-Stack Development

Each component of the full-stack serves an important function in delivering a complete web application.

Frontend Development

Frontend development is everything that users see and interact with on their web browsers. It includes:

- **HTML**: The structure of the web page.
- **CSS**: The design and layout of the web page.
- **JavaScript**: Adds interactivity and dynamic elements to the page (e.g., dropdown menus, animations).

Frontend developers ensure that users have an engaging and intuitive experience. They are concerned with making sure the site or app is visually appealing, functional, and easy to navigate.

Backend Development

The backend refers to everything that happens behind the scenes in an application. It handles:

- **Server**: The environment where your application lives.
- **Business Logic**: The code that makes decisions, such as user authentication or processing transactions.
- **API (Application Programming Interface)**: This allows the frontend to communicate with the backend, typically through HTTP requests (like GET, POST, PUT, DELETE).

Backend developers build the engine that powers the frontend experience. They ensure data is handled correctly, processes are automated, and users' requests are responded to appropriately.

Databases

Databases store the data that powers the app. There are two types of databases to consider:

- **Relational Databases** (e.g., MySQL, PostgreSQL) store data in tables and are useful for structured data with clear relationships between pieces of information.
- **NoSQL Databases** (e.g., MongoDB, Firebase) store data in a more flexible, document-based structure, making them ideal for unstructured or rapidly evolving data.

Databases are where all the core information lives: from user accounts to transaction details, product listings, and much more. They allow an app to store and retrieve data efficiently, ensuring that users always get the most up-to-date information.

JavaScript and TypeScript: Why TypeScript Matters in Full-Stack Development

Comparing JavaScript vs TypeScript

JavaScript has been the go-to language for web development for years. However, as applications grew more complex, developers needed a language that could help catch mistakes earlier in the development process. This is where **TypeScript** comes in.

JavaScript is a loosely-typed language, meaning you don't have to specify the type of data (such as numbers, strings, or objects) when defining variables. This makes JavaScript quick to write and flexible.

However, it also leads to issues when you try to scale an application or when debugging becomes tricky, as the types of variables are not explicitly defined.

TypeScript, on the other hand, is a **typed superset** of JavaScript. It introduces static types, which means you define what kind of data your variables will hold upfront. This helps catch errors at compile-time rather than at runtime, making debugging much easier.

Key Benefits of TypeScript:

- **Type Safety**: Prevents unexpected bugs by checking types at compile time.
- **Better Tooling**: Integrated support in IDEs and editors, like IntelliSense, making it easier to spot errors.
- **Scalability**: TypeScript's type system allows for better tooling as projects grow in size, making it easier to maintain large codebases.

Why Use TypeScript in Full-Stack Development?

For full-stack development, TypeScript ensures that both the frontend and backend are written with predictable, safe code. With the same language running on both ends, communication between the frontend (React) and backend (Node.js) becomes more seamless.

Additionally, when working with databases, TypeScript allows you to define types for the data models, which provides clarity and reduces the chances of runtime errors when accessing the database.

Setting Up Your Development Environment for TypeScript

Before diving into TypeScript, let's first set up the development environment. These are the key tools you'll need:

1. **Node.js**: Make sure Node.js is installed on your system. TypeScript works seamlessly with Node.js and npm (Node's package manager).
2. **Text Editor or IDE**: You'll need a code editor like **Visual Studio Code**, which has built-in TypeScript support and offers IntelliSense.
3. **TypeScript Compiler**: Install TypeScript globally with `npm install -g typescript` to compile your TypeScript files into JavaScript.
4. **Package Manager**: Use npm or yarn to manage your dependencies, such as React and Express.

Once you've installed these tools, create a project folder and initialize a new TypeScript project using the following commands:

```bash
bash
```

```bash
mkdir my-fullstack-project
cd my-fullstack-project
npm init -y
npm install typescript ts-node express react
```

You can now create your first **TypeScript configuration file** (`tsconfig.json`), which will control how TypeScript compiles your code.

Essential Tools and Frameworks for Full-Stack Development

In full-stack JavaScript development, there are a few key tools and frameworks that are commonly used to build, run, and deploy your applications. Let's look at them:

1. **Node.js**: The JavaScript runtime that powers the backend of your application.
2. **Express.js**: A minimalist web framework for Node.js. It simplifies routing, middleware, and request handling.
3. **React**: A JavaScript library for building interactive user interfaces, particularly for single-page applications (SPAs). React allows for efficient rendering of UI components.

4. **TypeScript**: As discussed, TypeScript adds type safety to JavaScript, helping to manage complex applications effectively.

5. **MongoDB**: A NoSQL database that's flexible and scales well with large data.

Why These Tools?

- **Node.js** and **Express** are incredibly fast and efficient for building APIs, handling HTTP requests, and processing server-side logic.

- **React** provides a powerful, reusable component model, making it easy to create interactive UIs that dynamically update without needing to refresh the page.

- **TypeScript** gives you stronger tooling and better predictability, which helps when working with larger applications or teams.

- **MongoDB** is used frequently in full-stack JavaScript applications due to its ease of use with JSON-like documents.

Real-World Example: A Simple App Integrating TypeScript with Node.js

Let's put everything together with a simple example. Imagine you're building a basic **to-do list application**. This app will allow users to add, delete, and update tasks. We'll use Node.js and Express for the backend and React for the frontend, all powered by TypeScript.

1. **Backend (Node.js + Express + TypeScript)**: We'll start by creating a simple API with Express to manage tasks. The server will handle HTTP requests for adding, deleting, and listing tasks.
2. **Frontend (React + TypeScript)**: We'll build a React app that allows the user to interact with the to-do list. The React app will send requests to the backend to add or delete tasks and update the UI dynamically.

Project Structure:

plaintext

```
/my-fullstack-app
  /frontend
    /src
      /components
      /App.tsx
  /backend
```

```
/src
  /controllers
  /models
  /server.ts
```

You will create routes in the backend for adding and deleting tasks, and on the frontend, display tasks using React components.

Chapter 2: Getting Started with Node.js

Understanding Node.js

What is Node.js?

Node.js is a powerful, open-source, cross-platform runtime environment that allows you to run JavaScript code on the server side. Traditionally, JavaScript was used only for frontend development—executed in the browser. However, with Node.js, JavaScript can now be used to build server-side applications, making it possible to create full-stack applications using a single language (JavaScript).

Node.js is built on the **V8 JavaScript engine**, the same engine that powers Google Chrome. It executes JavaScript code with high performance and efficiency, enabling non-blocking asynchronous operations.

Event-Driven Architecture

One of the key features of Node.js is its **event-driven architecture**. This means that instead of the program waiting for tasks like file I/O or network requests to complete (blocking), Node.js leverages an

event loop that handles these operations asynchronously. When a task is completed, an event is emitted, and the program can continue processing without waiting. This architecture enables Node.js to handle many concurrent connections efficiently, making it ideal for scalable network applications.

- **Non-Blocking I/O**: In a typical server, when the server receives a request for data (say, from a database or file), it waits for the data before continuing with other requests. In Node.js, I/O operations (like reading a file or querying a database) are non-blocking, meaning they are handled asynchronously. This improves performance, especially for applications that need to handle a large number of simultaneous requests.

- **Single-Threaded**: Despite being capable of handling many requests concurrently, Node.js operates on a single thread. It manages concurrency by using the event loop to handle multiple tasks efficiently without having multiple threads of execution running simultaneously.

How Does Node.js Fit Into Full-Stack Development?

In full-stack JavaScript development, Node.js plays the role of the **backend environment**. It enables the server to handle client requests, communicate with databases, and serve data to the frontend in a fast and efficient way.

Many modern applications rely on Node.js for backend services. Its event-driven nature makes it highly suitable for **real-time applications**, such as chat applications, gaming, or collaborative tools, where low latency and scalability are essential. Moreover, because Node.js is based on JavaScript, developers can use the same language for both the frontend (with frameworks like React or Angular) and the backend.

Setting Up Your Node.js Development Environment

Before you start writing Node.js applications, you'll need to set up the development environment. Here are the essential steps to get started:

1. **Installing Node.js and npm**:
   The first thing you need is to install **Node.js** and **npm** (Node Package Manager) on your machine. npm is a command-line tool that helps you manage JavaScript packages and dependencies.
   - Go to Node.js download page.
   - Download the latest stable version for your operating system (either LTS or Current).
   - After installation, check the versions to confirm:

```bash
node -v
npm -v
```

2. **Setting Up Your Project Folder**:

   Once Node.js is installed, you can create a directory for your Node.js project. This will hold all the files related to the project.

   ```bash
   mkdir my-node-app
   cd my-node-app
   ```

3. **Initializing a Node.js Project**:

   Use npm to initialize your project, which creates a `package.json` file. This file will store information about your app, including dependencies and scripts.

   ```bash
   npm init -y
   ```

   This will create a default `package.json` file, which is essential for managing your project's dependencies.

4. **Installing Essential Dependencies**:

   To begin developing with Node.js, you'll need several dependencies. Start by installing **Express,** a minimal web framework for Node.js, which makes it easier to build APIs and handle HTTP requests.

   ```bash
   npm install express
   ```

   You can also install other dependencies you might need for your project as you go along.

Your First Express Server

Now that you've set up your environment, let's create your first basic **Express server** using Node.js.

1. **Creating the Server**:

   In your project folder, create a file called `server.js`. This will be the main entry point for your application. Open the file in your code editor and add the following code to set up a basic Express server.

   ```javascript
   const express = require('express');
   ```

```
const app = express();

// Middleware to handle JSON requests
app.use(express.json());

// Basic route
app.get('/', (req, res) => {
  res.send('Hello, Node.js with Express!');
});

// Starting the server
const PORT = process.env.PORT || 3000;
app.listen(PORT, () => {
  console.log(`Server is running on port
${PORT}`);
});
```

2. **Understanding the Code**:

   o **express()**: This function creates an Express application instance.

   o **app.use(express.json())**: This middleware allows the server to parse incoming JSON data in HTTP requests.

   o **app.get()**: This defines a basic route that listens for GET requests to the root URL /.

   o **app.listen()**: This starts the server, listening for requests on a specified port (default: 3000).

3. **Running the Server**:

   Now, run the server using Node.js.

   ```bash
   bash
   ```

   ```bash
   node server.js
   ```

   You should see the message: `Server is running on port 3000.`

4. **Testing the Server**:

   Open a web browser or use a tool like **Postman** to navigate to `http://localhost:3000`. You should see the message: `Hello, Node.js with Express!.`

Hands-On Project: Build a Simple RESTful API with Node.js and TypeScript

Now that you've created a basic server, it's time to dive deeper by building a **RESTful API** with **Node.js** and **TypeScript**.

Step 1: Setting Up TypeScript in Your Project

1. **Install TypeScript**:

   Install TypeScript and the required types for Node.js and
   Express.

   bash

   ```
   npm install typescript @types/node
   @types/express --save-dev
   ```

2. **Initialize TypeScript Configuration**:

   Create a `tsconfig.json` file in your project folder.

   bash

   ```
   npx tsc --init
   ```

   This file controls how TypeScript compiles your code into
   JavaScript.

3. **Project Structure**:

   plaintext

   ```
   /src
     /controllers
       taskController.ts
     /models
   ```

```
task.ts

server.ts
```

Step 2: Creating the API Endpoints

In the `server.ts` file, you will set up basic routes to manage tasks.

typescript

```typescript
import express, { Request, Response } from 'express';
import { Task } from './models/task';

const app = express();
const PORT = 3000;

app.use(express.json());

const tasks: Task[] = [];

app.get('/tasks', (req: Request, res: Response) => {
  res.json(tasks);
});

app.post('/tasks', (req: Request, res: Response) => {
  const newTask = req.body;
  tasks.push(newTask);
  res.status(201).json(newTask);
});
```

```
app.delete('/tasks/:id', (req: Request, res:
Response) => {
  const taskId = parseInt(req.params.id);
  const taskIndex = tasks.findIndex(task => task.id
=== taskId);

  if (taskIndex !== -1) {
    tasks.splice(taskIndex, 1);
    res.status(200).json({ message: 'Task deleted
successfully' });
  } else {
    res.status(404).json({ message: 'Task not found'
});
  }
});

app.listen(PORT, () => {
  console.log(`Server is running on port ${PORT}`);
});
```

Step 3: Task Model (task.ts)

The `Task` model defines the structure of the task objects.

```
typescript
```

```typescript
export interface Task {
  id: number;
  title: string;
  completed: boolean;
}
```

```
}
```

Step 4: Running the API

To run the server, you need to compile the TypeScript code first:

```bash

npx tsc
```

Then, run the compiled JavaScript file with Node.js:

```bash

node dist/server.js
```

Testing the API

You can now test the API with Postman or any HTTP client:

- **GET** `http://localhost:3000/tasks`: Get all tasks.
- **POST** `http://localhost:3000/tasks`: Create a new task.
- **DELETE** `http://localhost:3000/tasks/{id}`: Delete a task by its ID.

Real-World Application: Understanding the Role of Node.js in Backend Services for eCommerce

Node.js plays a critical role in the backend of modern eCommerce platforms, providing scalability, speed, and flexibility. Here's how Node.js powers eCommerce:

1. **Handling Real-Time Transactions**:
   Node.js can manage high-frequency, low-latency transactions in real time, which is essential for eCommerce sites that need to process payments and inventory updates quickly.

2. **Scalability**:
   With its non-blocking, event-driven model, Node.js allows eCommerce applications to scale easily. Whether it's handling thousands of simultaneous customer requests or processing orders, Node.js can manage high concurrency without compromising performance.

3. **Handling APIs and Data Management**:
   eCommerce sites rely on APIs to interact with payment gateways, inventory systems, and customer data. Node.js handles these APIs efficiently, allowing seamless communication between different parts of the platform.

4. **Database Integration**:
   Node.js is commonly paired with databases like **MongoDB** or

MySQL in eCommerce applications. These databases store product details, customer information, and order history, and Node.js makes the retrieval and management of this data fast and efficient.

5. **Real-Time Updates**:

Real-time capabilities in Node.js make it an excellent choice for building eCommerce features like live order tracking, price updates, and customer support chat features.

Chapter 3: Building Robust APIs with Express and TypeScript

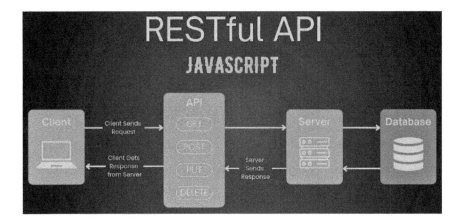

Introduction to REST APIs

What is a REST API?

A **REST API** (Representational State Transfer Application Programming Interface) is a set of rules and conventions that define how web services communicate over the internet. It allows different software systems to interact with each other, typically through HTTP requests such as **GET**, **POST**, **PUT**, and **DELETE**. These actions are used to perform operations on resources, which could be any object, such as user data, product listings, or images.

REST is based on the idea that the communication between the client and server is stateless, meaning that each request from a client to a server must contain all the necessary information for the server to fulfill the request. The server does not store any data about previous requests.

A REST API works by exposing **endpoints,** which are specific URLs that represent data and define how to interact with it. For example, a REST API for managing products might have the following endpoints:

- **GET /products** – Retrieves a list of products.
- **POST /products** – Adds a new product to the database.
- **PUT /products/{id}** – Updates an existing product.
- **DELETE /products/{id}** – Deletes a product.

Why Are REST APIs Important?

REST APIs are critical for modern web and mobile applications because they enable the exchange of data between the frontend (client) and backend (server) of applications. REST APIs are:

- **Stateless**: No client context is stored on the server, making it scalable and flexible.
- **Flexible**: REST APIs allow you to access various resources (e.g., data or services) over the web using HTTP methods.
- **Easy to Understand**: RESTful APIs are based on standard HTTP methods, which most developers are already familiar with.

- **Platform Independent**: REST APIs use standard protocols, so they can work with almost any programming language, making them language-agnostic.

In modern application development, APIs are an essential part of the architecture because they provide a way for different systems and services to communicate and exchange information.

Setting Up Express with TypeScript

Configuring Express to Work with TypeScript

Now that you understand the basics of REST APIs, let's dive into building one using **Express** and **TypeScript**. Express is a lightweight web framework for Node.js, commonly used to handle HTTP requests and responses. With TypeScript, we can add type safety and better tooling to our Express application.

Step 1: Initialize the Project

To start, let's create a new project directory and initialize it with npm.

```bash
mkdir express-ts-api
cd express-ts-api
```

```
npm init -y
```

This creates a `package.json` file, which will manage your project's dependencies.

Step 2: Install Dependencies

Next, you need to install **Express** and TypeScript along with the necessary type definitions to enable TypeScript support for Express.

```bash
bash
```

```
npm install express
npm install typescript @types/node @types/express --
save-dev
```

- **express**: The web framework used to build APIs.
- **typescript**: The language that provides type safety.
- **@types/node**: Type definitions for Node.js to help TypeScript understand Node's built-in modules.
- **@types/express**: Type definitions for Express to enable TypeScript to understand how to interact with Express.

Step 3: Set Up TypeScript Configuration

Now, initialize the TypeScript configuration file (`tsconfig.json`) that tells TypeScript how to compile the code.

```bash
npx tsc --init
```

This generates the `tsconfig.json` file. Make sure it includes the following settings:

```json
{
  "compilerOptions": {
    "target": "ES6",
    "module": "CommonJS",
    "strict": true,
    "esModuleInterop": true,
    "skipLibCheck": true,
    "forceConsistentCasingInFileNames": true,
    "outDir": "./dist"
  },
  "include": ["src/**/*.ts"]
}
```

- **"target": "ES6"**: Compiles TypeScript to modern JavaScript.
- **"module": "CommonJS"**: Specifies the module system used by Node.js.
- **"outDir": "./dist"**: Specifies the directory where the compiled JavaScript files will be placed.

Step 4: Project Structure

Here's the basic structure for the project:

plaintext

```
express-ts-api/
├── src/
│   ├── routes/
│   │   └── productRoutes.ts
│   ├── controllers/
│   │   └── productController.ts
│   ├── models/
│   │   └── product.ts
│   ├── app.ts
├── package.json
├── tsconfig.json
```

- **app.ts:** This file sets up the Express server and configuration.
- **routes/:** Contains the Express routes for your API.
- **controllers/:** Contains the logic to handle incoming requests.
- **models/:** Defines the structure of your data (e.g., product schema).

Middleware in Express

What is Middleware?

Middleware in Express refers to functions that sit in the request-response cycle, receiving the HTTP request, processing it, and passing it along to the next step in the cycle (either another middleware function or the final route handler). Middleware functions can perform tasks like:

- **Validating data**: Ensuring that requests have the right structure before continuing.
- **Logging**: Recording details about incoming requests.
- **Authentication**: Verifying user identity before allowing access to certain endpoints.

Creating Custom Middleware in Express

Let's create a simple middleware function that logs each incoming request's HTTP method and URL.

In `src/middleware/logger.ts`:

```typescript
import { Request, Response, NextFunction } from 'express';
```

```typescript
const logger = (req: Request, res: Response, next:
NextFunction) => {
  console.log(`[${new Date().toISOString()}]
${req.method} ${req.url}`);
  next(); // Pass control to the next middleware or
route handler
};


export default logger;
```

Now, integrate this middleware into the Express app by adding it in app.ts:

typescript

```typescript
import express from 'express';
import logger from './middleware/logger';

const app = express();

// Use the logger middleware for all incoming
requests
app.use(logger);

app.get('/', (req, res) => {
  res.send('Hello, World!');
});

const PORT = 3000;
```

```
app.listen(PORT, () => {
  console.log(`Server running on port ${PORT}`);
});
```

This middleware will log every request's method and URL to the console, helping track traffic through your API.

Hands-On Project: Build a CRUD API Using TypeScript and Express

Now, let's create a basic CRUD (Create, Read, Update, Delete) API that manages **products**. Each product will have a name, price, and description.

Step 1: Define the Product Model

In `src/models/product.ts`, create a TypeScript interface for the product.

typescript

```
export interface Product {
  id: number;
  name: string;
  price: number;
  description: string;
```

```
}
```

Step 2: Create the Controller

The controller will handle business logic for interacting with products. Create `src/controllers/productController.ts`.

typescript

```typescript
import { Request, Response } from 'express';
import { Product } from '../models/product';

// Sample in-memory database
let products: Product[] = [
  { id: 1, name: 'Laptop', price: 999.99,
description: 'A high performance laptop' },
  { id: 2, name: 'Phone', price: 699.99, description:
'A feature-rich smartphone' }
];

export const getProducts = (req: Request, res:
Response) => {
  res.json(products);
};

export const createProduct = (req: Request, res:
Response) => {
  const { name, price, description } = req.body;
  const newProduct: Product = { id: products.length +
1, name, price, description };
```

```
  products.push(newProduct);
  res.status(201).json(newProduct);
};


export const updateProduct = (req: Request, res:
Response) => {
  const { id } = req.params;
  const { name, price, description } = req.body;

  const product = products.find(p => p.id ===
parseInt(id));
  if (product) {
    product.name = name || product.name;
    product.price = price || product.price;
    product.description = description ||
product.description;
    res.json(product);
  } else {
    res.status(404).json({ message: 'Product not
found' });
  }
};


export const deleteProduct = (req: Request, res:
Response) => {
  const { id } = req.params;
  products = products.filter(p => p.id !==
parseInt(id));
  res.status(204).send();
```

```
};
```

Step 3: Define Routes

In `src/routes/productRoutes.ts`, define the routes for the API.

```typescript
import { Router } from 'express';
import { getProducts, createProduct, updateProduct,
deleteProduct } from
'../controllers/productController';

const router = Router();

router.get('/products', getProducts);
router.post('/products', createProduct);
router.put('/products/:id', updateProduct);
router.delete('/products/:id', deleteProduct);

export default router;
```

Step 4: Set Up the App

Finally, in `src/app.ts`, set up the server and use the routes.

```typescript
import express from 'express';
import productRoutes from './routes/productRoutes';
```

```
const app = express();
app.use(express.json());

app.use('/api', productRoutes);

const PORT = 3000;
app.listen(PORT, () => {
  console.log(`Server running on port ${PORT}`);
});
```

Step 5: Test the API

1. **GET** `http://localhost:3000/api/products` – Retrieves all products.
2. **POST** `http://localhost:3000/api/products` – Adds a new product.
3. **PUT** `http://localhost:3000/api/products/{id}` – Updates an existing product.
4. **DELETE** `http://localhost:3000/api/products/{id}` – Deletes a product.

Real-World Application: Build an API for a Content Management System

In a content management system (CMS), an API is needed to manage users, posts, comments, and other entities. This can be broken down into several endpoints that manage each part of the system.

The process for building a CMS API is very similar to the CRUD API above. You will define models (e.g., for users, posts, comments), create controllers to handle business logic, and set up routes to interact with the data.

For instance, you could have the following endpoints in a CMS:

- **GET /posts**: Retrieve all blog posts.
- **POST /posts**: Create a new blog post.
- **PUT /posts/{id}**: Update an existing post.
- **DELETE /posts/{id}**: Delete a blog post.

By extending the previous hands-on project and adding more functionality, such as authentication and permissions, you can build a robust API for a CMS.

Chapter 4: Introduction to React and Frontend Development

What is React?

React is a powerful and widely-used JavaScript library for building user interfaces, particularly for **single-page applications (SPAs)**. Developed by **Facebook**, React allows developers to create complex UIs through the use of simple, reusable components. One of its most significant advantages is its ability to efficiently update and render the correct component when data changes, thanks to its **virtual DOM** and **reactive programming** model.

React is focused on the **view layer** in the **Model-View-Controller (MVC)** architecture. While it doesn't include everything needed for full application development (like routing or state management), it pairs well with other libraries and frameworks to create a full-stack solution. This modular approach allows developers to pick and choose the best tools for their needs.

The Components-Based Architecture

The core of React is its **component-based architecture**. Components are like building blocks for the user interface. They are reusable, independent pieces of the UI that can be composed together to create a complex application.

Components in React are typically written as JavaScript **functions** or **classes** and can manage their own state and lifecycle methods. There are two types of components in React:

1. **Functional Components**: These are stateless components, typically used for simpler components that don't manage their own state but can receive props and render output.
2. **Class Components**: These components can manage their own state and contain lifecycle methods that enable them to perform specific actions at various points in the component's lifecycle.

React also has a feature called **JSX** (JavaScript XML), which allows developers to write HTML-like code within JavaScript. JSX allows for a more declarative and intuitive approach to rendering UI elements.

Key Features of React's Component-Based Architecture:

- **Reusability**: Once a component is built, it can be reused in other parts of the application, which promotes clean, DRY (Don't Repeat Yourself) code.

- **Separation of Concerns**: Each component manages a specific part of the UI, making the application easier to scale and maintain.
- **Declarative UI**: With React, you describe how the UI should look based on the current state, and React takes care of rendering and updating it accordingly.

Setting Up React with TypeScript

To build a modern, robust application with React and TypeScript, the first step is setting up your development environment. TypeScript enhances React by providing type safety, making the code more predictable and less error-prone.

Step 1: Setting Up the Project

Let's start by creating a new React project using **Create React App**, a tool that sets up everything you need for a React application.

1. **Install Create React App** with TypeScript template:

    bash

    ```bash
    npx create-react-app my-react-app --template
    typescript
    ```

This command will create a new project named `my-react-app` and set up the necessary files for TypeScript integration.

2. **Install Additional Dependencies** (Optional):

   If you plan to use state management libraries like Redux, or routing libraries like React Router, you can install them:

   bash

   ```
   npm install redux react-redux react-router-dom
   ```

3. **Running the App**:

   Once the setup is complete, navigate to the project directory and run the development server:

   bash

   ```
   cd my-react-app
   npm start
   ```

   Your React application will now be running locally at `http://localhost:3000/`.

Step 2: Understanding the Folder Structure

A typical React + TypeScript project setup will look like this:

```plaintext

my-react-app/
├── public/
│   └── index.html
├── src/
│   ├── assets/
│   ├── components/
│   ├── App.tsx
│   ├── index.tsx
│   ├── App.css
├── tsconfig.json
```

- **public/index.html**: The base HTML file where the React app is rendered.
- **src/index.tsx**: The entry point for the React app. This is where React hooks into the DOM.
- **src/App.tsx**: A React component that serves as the main container of your app.

Understanding JSX, Components, and Props

React's declarative nature is built around **JSX, components**, and **props**. Let's dive into these core concepts.

JSX (JavaScript XML)

JSX is a syntax extension for JavaScript, allowing you to write HTML-like code within JavaScript. It enables React to define UI elements in a declarative way.

For example, a basic JSX component could look like this:

tsx

```
const Greeting: React.FC = () => {
  return <h1>Hello, welcome to my React app!</h1>;
};
```

JSX code is ultimately converted to `React.createElement()` calls under the hood, which makes it possible for React to efficiently manage updates to the DOM.

Components in React

As mentioned earlier, components are the heart of React. A component can be a simple UI element like a button, or a more complex entity like an entire page. Components allow developers to break down the user interface into smaller, reusable parts.

Here's an example of a **Functional Component** in React:

tsx

```
const Button: React.FC = () => {
  return <button>Click Me</button>;
};
```

This button component can now be used in other parts of the application by simply referencing it:

tsx

```
const App: React.FC = () => {
  return (
    <div>
      <Button />
      <Button />
    </div>
  );
};
```

Props in React

Props (short for properties) are how data is passed to components in React. They allow components to be dynamic and flexible, rendering different content based on the data passed to them.

For example, you can pass a `name` prop to a component to customize its content:

tsx

```
interface GreetingProps {
  name: string;
}

const Greeting: React.FC<GreetingProps> = ({ name })
=> {
  return <h1>Hello, {name}!</h1>;
};

const App: React.FC = () => {
  return <Greeting name="John" />;
};
```

In this example, `Greeting` is a component that accepts a `name` prop, and the content changes dynamically based on the passed value.

Hands-On Project: Build a React Component that Interacts with Your Node.js API

Now that we've covered the basics of React, let's build a practical example. In this hands-on project, we'll build a React component that interacts with the Node.js API you built in Chapter 2. The goal is to **fetch data from the Node.js API** and display it in a list on the frontend.

Step 1: Set Up the React Component

First, let's create a new component called **ProductList**. This component will make an API call to the Node.js API to retrieve a list of products.

In `src/components/ProductList.tsx`:

tsx

```tsx
import React, { useEffect, useState } from 'react';

interface Product {
  id: number;
  name: string;
  price: number;
  description: string;
}

const ProductList: React.FC = () => {
  const [products, setProducts] =
useState<Product[]>([]);
  const [loading, setLoading] =
useState<boolean>(true);

  useEffect(() => {
    fetch('http://localhost:3000/api/products')
      .then(response => response.json())
      .then(data => {
```

```
      setProducts(data);
      setLoading(false);
    })
    .catch(error => {
      console.error('Error fetching products:',
error);
      setLoading(false);
    });
  }, []);

  return (
    <div>
      {loading ? (
        <p>Loading products...</p>
      ) : (
        <ul>
          {products.map(product => (
            <li key={product.id}>
              <h2>{product.name}</h2>
              <p>{product.description}</p>
              <p>Price: ${product.price}</p>
            </li>
          ))}
        </ul>
      )}
    </div>
  );
};
```

```
export default ProductList;
```

This component fetches the list of products from the backend using the `fetch()` method and displays them in a simple list.

Step 2: Use the Component in the App

In `src/App.tsx`, use the `ProductList` component to display the products:

tsx

```
import React from 'react';
import ProductList from './components/ProductList';

const App: React.FC = () => {
  return (
    <div>
      <h1>Product List</h1>
      <ProductList />
    </div>
  );
};

export default App;
```

Step 3: Running the Project

Make sure your Node.js server is running, and then start the React development server:

bash

```
npm start
```

Your React app should now be able to fetch and display products from the Node.js API.

Real-World Application: How React Powers Modern Single-Page Applications

React is a popular choice for building **Single-Page Applications (SPAs),** where the entire user interface is loaded once, and only the necessary parts of the page are updated when the data changes. This approach leads to a smoother user experience, as there is no need to reload the entire page when navigating between different views.

Why SPAs?

1. **Faster Performance**: SPAs provide a more responsive experience since only the relevant data and components are updated.
2. **Reduced Server Load**: SPAs often use client-side routing, reducing the number of requests made to the server.
3. **Better User Experience**: Because of the seamless transitions, SPAs provide a more app-like experience.

React's component-based architecture is perfectly suited to SPAs because each component can manage its state and render independently based on the data it receives.

React in the Real World

- **Facebook**: React was developed by Facebook and powers the Facebook website, making the user experience faster and more dynamic.
- **Instagram**: Instagram uses React to provide users with smooth navigation between the feed, profile, and messaging features.
- **Netflix**: Netflix uses React to build its complex frontend, which requires handling large amounts of data and ensuring a smooth, engaging experience for users.

Chapter 5: Advanced React Features

React Hooks: useState, useEffect, and Custom Hooks

Introduction to React Hooks

React introduced **hooks** in version 16.8 as a way to allow functional components to manage state and side effects, something that was previously only possible in class components. Hooks provide a cleaner and more concise way to manage state, lifecycle methods, and other React features in functional components.

In earlier versions of React, developers had to rely on class components to handle things like local component state, lifecycle methods, and side effects. Hooks enable functional components to handle all these things without needing to convert them into class components.

The most commonly used React hooks are:

1. **useState**: Allows you to add state to functional components.
2. **useEffect**: Enables you to perform side effects in functional components.
3. **Custom Hooks**: Lets you extract and reuse logic across multiple components.

useState: Managing State in Functional Components

The `useState` hook allows functional components to store and manage state in a way that was previously only possible with class components. It returns an array with two elements: the current state value and a function to update that state.

Syntax:

tsx

```
const [state, setState] = useState(initialValue);
```

- **state**: The current value of the state.
- **setState**: A function that updates the value of the state.

- **initialValue**: The initial state value.

Here's a basic example of how `useState` works:

tsx

```tsx
import React, { useState } from 'react';

const Counter: React.FC = () => {
  const [count, setCount] = useState(0);

  const increment = () => setCount(count + 1);
  const decrement = () => setCount(count - 1);

  return (
    <div>
      <h1>Counter: {count}</h1>
      <button onClick={increment}>Increase</button>
      <button onClick={decrement}>Decrease</button>
    </div>
  );
};

export default Counter;
```

In this example, the `count` state is initialized to 0, and the `setCount` function is used to update it when the user clicks the buttons.

useEffect: Handling Side Effects in React

The `useEffect` hook is used to perform side effects in your components. A side effect is any operation that occurs in a component that doesn't directly involve rendering or returning JSX. Examples include data fetching, DOM manipulations, and setting up subscriptions or timers.

Syntax:

```tsx
useEffect(() => {
  // Code to run when the component mounts or updates
}, [dependencies]);
```

- The **callback function** is executed after the render.
- The **dependencies array** specifies when the effect should run. If you pass an empty array `[]`, the effect will only run once when the component mounts.

Here's an example that fetches data from an API using `useEffect`:

```tsx
import React, { useState, useEffect } from 'react';

const FetchData: React.FC = () => {
```

```
  const [data, setData] = useState(null);

  useEffect(() => {

fetch('https://jsonplaceholder.typicode.com/posts')
      .then(response => response.json())
      .then(json => setData(json));
  }, []);

  if (!data) return <p>Loading...</p>;

  return (
    <div>
      <h2>Posts</h2>
      <ul>
        {data.map((post: { id: number, title: string
}) => (
          <li key={post.id}>{post.title}</li>
        ))}
      </ul>
    </div>
  );
};

export default FetchData;
```

In this example, `useEffect` runs when the component mounts and fetches data from an API. The data is then stored in the `data` state using `setData`.

Custom Hooks: Reusing Logic Across Components

Custom hooks are a powerful feature of React that allow you to encapsulate logic and share it between multiple components. Custom hooks are simply JavaScript functions that start with the word use and can use other React hooks inside them.

For example, you can create a custom hook for managing a counter:

tsx

```tsx
import { useState } from 'react';

function useCounter(initialValue: number = 0) {
  const [count, setCount] = useState(initialValue);

  const increment = () => setCount(count + 1);
  const decrement = () => setCount(count - 1);

  return { count, increment, decrement };
}

export default useCounter;
```

Then you can use this custom hook in any component:

tsx

```
import React from 'react';
import useCounter from './useCounter';

const CounterComponent: React.FC = () => {
  const { count, increment, decrement } =
useCounter();

  return (
    <div>
      <h1>Counter: {count}</h1>
      <button onClick={increment}>Increase</button>
      <button onClick={decrement}>Decrease</button>
    </div>
  );
};

export default CounterComponent;
```

Custom hooks let you extract common logic (like handling state or fetching data) into reusable functions, reducing redundancy and making your code more maintainable.

State Management in React

State Management with Context API

In React, state can be managed locally within components using `useState`. However, as an application grows, passing state down through multiple layers of components (also known as "prop drilling") can become cumbersome. To solve this, React provides the **Context API**, which allows you to share state across your entire component tree without having to pass props down manually at every level.

To create a context:

tsx

```
import React, { createContext, useState, useContext }
from 'react';

interface AuthContextType {
  isAuthenticated: boolean;
  login: () => void;
  logout: () => void;
}

const AuthContext = createContext<AuthContextType |
undefined>(undefined);
```

```
const AuthProvider: React.FC = ({ children }) => {
  const [isAuthenticated, setIsAuthenticated] =
useState(false);

  const login = () => setIsAuthenticated(true);
  const logout = () => setIsAuthenticated(false);

  return (
    <AuthContext.Provider value={{ isAuthenticated,
login, logout }}>
      {children}
    </AuthContext.Provider>
  );
};

const useAuth = (): AuthContextType => {
  const context = useContext(AuthContext);
  if (!context) {
    throw new Error('useAuth must be used within an
AuthProvider');
  }
  return context;
};

export { AuthProvider, useAuth };
```

Then, wrap your root component with the AuthProvider in

App.tsx:

tsx

```tsx
import React from 'react';
import { AuthProvider } from './AuthContext';
import LoginButton from './LoginButton';

const App: React.FC = () => (
  <AuthProvider>
    <LoginButton />
  </AuthProvider>
);

export default App;
```

In `LoginButton.tsx`, you can now access and modify the state through the `useAuth` hook:

tsx

```tsx
import React from 'react';
import { useAuth } from './AuthContext';

const LoginButton: React.FC = () => {
  const { isAuthenticated, login, logout } =
useAuth();

  return (
    <div>
      {isAuthenticated ? (
```

```
        <button onClick={logout}>Logout</button>
      ) : (
        <button onClick={login}>Login</button>
      )}
    </div>
  );
};
```

```
export default LoginButton;
```

This allows you to share the `isAuthenticated` state across any component that needs it, without having to pass it down via props.

State Management with Redux

For larger applications with more complex state, **Redux** is a popular state management library that helps manage the state of your app in a centralized store. Redux stores the state in a single object, and components can access and modify it using **actions** and **reducers**.

To use Redux with React:

1. Install Redux and React-Redux:

   bash

   ```bash
   npm install redux react-redux
   ```

2. Create a Redux store, actions, and reducers.

3. Use `Provider` to pass the store to your app:

```tsx
import React from 'react';
import { Provider } from 'react-redux';
import store from './store';
import MyComponent from './MyComponent';

const App: React.FC = () => (
  <Provider store={store}>
    <MyComponent />
  </Provider>
);

export default App;
```

Redux is especially useful for managing global state, handling complex updates, and synchronizing state between components.

Forms and Validation in React

Handling Form Data

In React, form data is usually managed with state. You use the `useState` hook to keep track of the data entered into the form fields. Here's an example of a simple form that tracks the input:

```tsx
import React, { useState } from 'react';

const ContactForm: React.FC = () => {
  const [name, setName] = useState('');
  const [email, setEmail] = useState('');

  const handleSubmit = (e: React.FormEvent) => {
    e.preventDefault();
    console.log(`Name: ${name}, Email: ${email}`);
  };

  return (
    <form onSubmit={handleSubmit}>
      <input
        type="text"
        placeholder="Name"
        value={name}
        onChange={(e) => setName(e.target.value)}
      />
      <input
        type="email"
        placeholder="Email"
        value={email}
        onChange={(e) => setEmail(e.target.value)}
      />
      <button type="submit">Submit</button>
    </form>
```

```
    );
};
```

```
export default ContactForm;
```

Validating Form Data

To validate form inputs, you can write a function that checks if the entered values are correct. For example, to validate the email format:

tsx

```
const validateEmail = (email: string) => {
   const regex = /^[a-zA-Z0-9._-]+@[a-zA-Z0-9.-]+\.[a-zA-Z]{2,6}$/;
   return regex.test(email);
};
```

You can then use this function inside your form to check if the email entered is valid.

Hands-On Project: Create a Form in React that Sends Data to an Express API

In this project, you will create a form in React that allows users to submit their contact information (name and email) and send this data to an **Express API**.

Step 1: Create the Form Component

Create a form in React with input fields for name and email, and a submit button. Use state to store the values of the form fields and handle changes using `onChange`.

Step 2: Send Data to Express API

Use `fetch` or `axios` to send the form data to the backend API. The backend will handle the request, process the data, and send a response back to the frontend.

tsx

```tsx
import React, { useState } from 'react';

const ContactForm: React.FC = () => {
  const [name, setName] = useState('');
  const [email, setEmail] = useState('');
```

```
  const handleSubmit = async (e: React.FormEvent) =>
{
    e.preventDefault();

    const data = { name, email };

    try {
      const response = await
fetch('http://localhost:3000/api/contact', {
        method: 'POST',
        headers: { 'Content-Type': 'application/json'
},
        body: JSON.stringify(data),
      });

      const result = await response.json();
      console.log(result);
    } catch (error) {
      console.error('Error:', error);
    }
  };

  return (
    <form onSubmit={handleSubmit}>
      <input
        type="text"
        placeholder="Name"
        value={name}
        onChange={(e) => setName(e.target.value)}
```

```
      />
      <input
        type="email"
        placeholder="Email"
        value={email}
        onChange={(e) => setEmail(e.target.value)}
      />
      <button type="submit">Submit</button>
    </form>
  );
};

export default ContactForm;
```

Real-World Application: How React and State Management Are Used in eCommerce Sites

React is widely used in **eCommerce websites** due to its fast performance, ability to manage dynamic content, and modularity. Many eCommerce platforms rely on React for:

1. **Product Listings**: React can render lists of products dynamically as users interact with filters and sort options.
2. **Shopping Cart**: Managing the cart's state and updating it in real-time.
3. **User Authentication**: Using React to manage user login, registration, and authentication states.

State management with tools like **Redux** or **Context API** is essential in large-scale eCommerce sites. For example, when a user adds a product to the cart, the cart's state needs to be updated across different parts of the site. By using Redux or Context API, this state can be shared and accessed by multiple components across the application.

Chapter 6: Connecting Frontend and Backend with API Calls

What is API Consumption?

API Consumption refers to the process of a frontend application requesting and receiving data from a backend API. In modern web development, the frontend (client-side) and backend (server-side) typically communicate via **APIs** (Application Programming Interfaces), which provide an interface for interacting with databases, performing business logic, and returning data to the frontend.

APIs are crucial for modern web applications because they decouple the frontend from the backend. This means the backend can evolve independently, and the frontend can be updated or replaced without affecting the underlying API. This separation of concerns allows for cleaner code, easier maintenance, and greater scalability.

When building applications, **API consumption** allows the frontend to retrieve data, submit forms, or even trigger actions on the server. For example, when a user logs in or submits a contact form, the frontend sends data to the backend API, which processes it and returns a response.

In a **React app**, API consumption typically happens using **AJAX (Asynchronous JavaScript and XML)**, a technology that allows for sending and receiving data asynchronously without refreshing the web page. This makes web applications more dynamic and interactive, providing a smooth user experience.

The process of API consumption is often broken down into several steps:

1. The frontend sends an HTTP request to the backend API.
2. The backend processes the request and performs necessary operations (e.g., querying a database).
3. The backend sends an HTTP response, typically in the form of JSON or XML.
4. The frontend processes the response and updates the user interface.

Fetching Data with Axios and Fetch

When consuming APIs in a React application, you need a way to make HTTP requests to the backend. The two most common methods to do this are **Axios** and **Fetch**.

What is Fetch?

`Fetch` is a native JavaScript function built into modern browsers that allows you to make network requests. It's a simple and promise-based API for fetching resources across the network. Fetch is built into the browser, so you don't need to install anything to use it.

Basic Syntax of Fetch:

```javascript
fetch(url, options)
  .then(response => response.json())  // Convert
response to JSON
  .then(data => console.log(data))    // Process the
data
  .catch(error => console.log('Error:', error));  //
Handle any errors
```

- **url**: The URL of the resource you're fetching.
- **options**: Optional settings (e.g., HTTP method, headers, body) to configure the request.

Example of Fetch in React:

```tsx
import React, { useState, useEffect } from 'react';
```

```
const PostList: React.FC = () => {
  const [posts, setPosts] = useState([]);
  const [loading, setLoading] = useState(true);

  useEffect(() => {

fetch('https://jsonplaceholder.typicode.com/posts')
      .then(response => response.json())
      .then(data => {
        setPosts(data);
        setLoading(false);
      })
      .catch(error => {
        console.error('Error fetching data:', error);
        setLoading(false);
      });
  }, []);

  if (loading) return <p>Loading posts...</p>;

  return (
    <div>
      <h2>Posts</h2>
      <ul>
        {posts.map(post => (
          <li key={post.id}>{post.title}</li>
        ))}
      </ul>
```

```
    </div>
  );
};
```

```
export default PostList;
```

In this example, the `fetch` function retrieves a list of posts from an API and displays them in the component. The `useEffect` hook ensures the data is fetched once the component is mounted, and the `useState` hook stores the fetched data.

What is Axios?

`Axios` is a promise-based JavaScript library for making HTTP requests, and it provides an easier, more flexible API compared to `fetch`. Axios has a lot of advantages over `fetch`, such as better handling of errors, automatic JSON parsing, and support for older browsers.

To use Axios, you first need to install it:

```
bash
```

```
npm install axios
```

Basic Syntax of Axios:

```javascript
javascript

axios.get(url)
  .then(response => console.log(response.data))    //
Process the response
  .catch(error => console.error('Error:', error));
// Handle errors
```

Axios supports all HTTP methods (GET, POST, PUT, DELETE, etc.), and it's much easier to use when dealing with complex requests, especially if you need to send data in the request body.

Example of Axios in React:

```tsx
tsx

import React, { useState, useEffect } from 'react';
import axios from 'axios';

const PostList: React.FC = () => {
  const [posts, setPosts] = useState([]);
  const [loading, setLoading] = useState(true);

  useEffect(() => {

axios.get('https://jsonplaceholder.typicode.com/posts')
      .then(response => {
        setPosts(response.data);
```

```
      setLoading(false);
    })
    .catch(error => {
      console.error('Error fetching data:', error);
      setLoading(false);
    });
}, []);

if (loading) return <p>Loading posts...</p>;

return (
  <div>
    <h2>Posts</h2>
    <ul>
      {posts.map(post => (
        <li key={post.id}>{post.title}</li>
      ))}
    </ul>
  </div>
);
};

export default PostList;
```

Axios simplifies many tasks, like handling request and response transformations, handling errors more easily, and sending requests with additional features like timeouts or cancellations.

Comparing Axios vs Fetch: When to Use Them

Feature	Axios	Fetch
Browser Support	Works across all modern browsers and IE11+	Works in most modern browsers (not in Internet Explorer)
Error Handling	Automatically rejects on HTTP errors (e.g., 404, 500)	Does not reject on HTTP errors, requires manual checking
Request Timeout	Supports timeout configurations easily	No built-in support for timeouts
Request Interception	Supports request and response interceptors	Not built-in; needs additional setup
Data Transformation	Automatic JSON data transformation	Needs manual transformation (`response.json()`)
Browser Compatibility	Works seamlessly in older browsers	More modern and not supported in older browsers

- **When to use Axios**: If you need more advanced features like interceptors, automatic transformation of JSON data, or the ability to cancel requests, Axios is the preferred choice.

- **When to use Fetch**: If you are working on a simpler project where browser support isn't a major concern, or if you want a native solution with fewer dependencies, `fetch` is sufficient.

Handling Errors and Responses

When fetching data from an API, it's important to handle errors gracefully. Both `fetch` and `axios` offer ways to catch errors, but their behavior differs slightly.

Handling Errors with Axios

Axios automatically throws an error for non-2xx status codes (e.g., 404, 500), making error handling easier. You can catch these errors using the `catch` block:

tsx

```tsx
axios.get('https://jsonplaceholder.typicode.com/posts')
  .then(response => {
    // Handle successful response
    console.log(response.data);
  })
  .catch(error => {
    // Handle errors
```

```
    if (error.response) {
      // The server responded with a status code
outside the range of 2xx
      console.error('Error response:',
error.response);
    } else if (error.request) {
      // The request was made but no response was
received
      console.error('Error request:', error.request);
    } else {
      // Other errors
      console.error('Error message:', error.message);
    }
  });
```

Handling Errors with Fetch

With `fetch`, errors are not automatically thrown for HTTP errors (like 404). You need to manually check if the response is successful (i.e., status code 2xx). If it's not, you can throw an error.

tsx

```
fetch('https://jsonplaceholder.typicode.com/posts')
  .then(response => {
    if (!response.ok) {
      throw new Error('Network response was not ok');
    }
    return response.json();
  })
```

```
.then(data => {
    console.log(data);
})
.catch(error => {
    console.error('There was a problem with the fetch
operation:', error);
});
```

In both cases, it's crucial to inform the user or log the issue if the request fails, providing them with a better experience and insight into what went wrong.

Hands-On Project: Fetch Data from Your Express API and Display it in React

In this hands-on project, you will connect a React frontend to an **Express API** by fetching data using **Axios** or **Fetch**.

Step 1: Setting Up the Express API

In server.js (from Chapter 2), set up a basic Express API that serves a list of products:

javascript

```
const express = require('express');
```

```
const app = express();
const PORT = 3000;

const products = [
  { id: 1, name: 'Laptop', price: 999 },
  { id: 2, name: 'Phone', price: 599 },
  { id: 3, name: 'Tablet', price: 399 }
];

app.get('/api/products', (req, res) => {
  res.json(products);
});

app.listen(PORT, () => {
  console.log(`Server running on
http://localhost:${PORT}`);
});
```

Step 2: Fetching Data in React

In your React app, use Axios or Fetch to fetch the products from your Express API and display them:

tsx

```
import React, { useState, useEffect } from 'react';
import axios from 'axios';

const ProductList: React.FC = () => {
  const [products, setProducts] = useState([]);
```

```
const [loading, setLoading] = useState(true);

useEffect(() => {
  axios.get('http://localhost:3000/api/products')
    .then(response => {
      setProducts(response.data);
      setLoading(false);
    })
    .catch(error => {
      console.error('Error fetching data:', error);
      setLoading(false);
    });
}, []);

if (loading) return <p>Loading products...</p>;

return (
  <div>
    <h2>Product List</h2>
    <ul>
      {products.map(product => (
        <li key={product.id}>
          {product.name} - ${product.price}
        </li>
      ))}
    </ul>
  </div>
);
};
```

```
export default ProductList;
```

Real-World Application: How Data Fetching Works in Modern Social Media Platforms

In modern social media platforms like **Facebook**, **Instagram**, and **Twitter**, data fetching is crucial to providing users with real-time content. These platforms rely heavily on APIs to dynamically load posts, comments, user profiles, and more.

1. **Infinite Scrolling**: Social media platforms often use infinite scrolling to load new posts or comments when a user reaches the bottom of the page. This is achieved by making API calls to fetch additional content when needed.

2. **Real-Time Updates**: To provide a dynamic, real-time experience, APIs are often used in combination with technologies like **WebSockets** or **Server-Sent Events (SSE)** to push updates to the frontend. For example, when someone likes or comments on a post, the frontend can automatically update without requiring the user to refresh the page.

3. **Pagination**: Social media platforms paginate large data sets (like posts) to prevent overwhelming the user or the server.

The API returns only a subset of the data, and the client can request more as needed.

Chapter 7: Databases in Full-Stack JavaScript Development

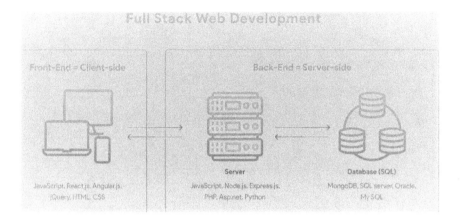

Choosing the Right Database for Your App

When developing a full-stack JavaScript application, choosing the right database is crucial for the performance, scalability, and maintainability of your project. Databases are used to store and manage your application's data, and selecting the right type of database for your app's needs can have a significant impact on its success.

The two main types of databases you'll encounter in full-stack development are **Relational Databases (RDBMS)** and **Non-relational Databases (NoSQL).**

Relational Databases (RDBMS)

Relational databases store data in tables, with rows representing records and columns representing attributes. They are highly structured and use **Structured Query Language (SQL)** to interact with the data. RDBMSs are well-suited for applications that require complex queries, transactions, and data consistency. Common examples of relational databases include:

- **MySQL**
- **PostgreSQL**
- **SQLite**

Key Features of RDBMS:

- **Data Integrity**: RDBMSs ensure data consistency using constraints like primary keys, foreign keys, and unique indexes.
- **ACID Transactions**: Relational databases support ACID properties (Atomicity, Consistency, Isolation, Durability), ensuring that operations like transfers or updates are reliable.
- **Structured Schema**: RDBMSs have a predefined schema, which means the structure of the data is defined before storing any data.

When to Use an RDBMS:

- When your data is structured, and you need to handle relationships between entities (e.g., users, orders, payments).
- When your application requires complex querying and joins across multiple tables.
- When you need strong consistency and reliable transactions.

Non-relational Databases (NoSQL)

Non-relational databases, also known as **NoSQL** databases, store data in formats like JSON, documents, key-value pairs, graphs, or wide-column stores. These databases are more flexible than relational databases, as they do not require a predefined schema, allowing developers to store data without worrying about its structure upfront.

Examples of non-relational databases include:

- **MongoDB** (Document store)
- **Cassandra** (Wide-column store)
- **Redis** (Key-value store)
- **Neo4j** (Graph database)

Key Features of NoSQL:

- **Flexible Schema**: NoSQL databases don't enforce a fixed schema, which allows you to store unstructured data or data that evolves over time.
- **Scalability**: NoSQL databases are designed for horizontal scaling, meaning they can distribute data across multiple servers.
- **Speed**: They offer high performance for read-heavy or write-heavy workloads.

When to Use a NoSQL Database:

- When your application's data is semi-structured or unstructured, such as user-generated content, logs, or sensor data.
- When your application needs to scale horizontally or handle large amounts of unstructured data.
- When you require rapid development and need a flexible schema to handle frequent changes to the data model.

Setting Up MongoDB with Node.js and TypeScript

MongoDB is one of the most popular NoSQL databases, often used in full-stack JavaScript applications. It is a document-based database that stores data in flexible **JSON-like** documents called

BSON (Binary JSON). MongoDB is highly scalable, flexible, and works well with large amounts of unstructured data.

To integrate MongoDB with a Node.js backend, you will need to install **MongoDB** and the **Mongoose** library, which provides an easier and more structured way of working with MongoDB in a Node.js application.

Step 1: Install MongoDB

Before setting up MongoDB, you'll need to install it locally or use a cloud database service like **MongoDB Atlas**.

To install MongoDB locally:

1. Visit the MongoDB Download Center.
2. Choose the appropriate version for your operating system.
3. Follow the instructions to install MongoDB on your machine.

Alternatively, if you prefer to use a cloud service, sign up for **MongoDB Atlas**, which provides a fully managed MongoDB database.

Step 2: Install Mongoose

To interact with MongoDB using Node.js and TypeScript, we will use **Mongoose**, an ODM (Object Document Mapper) library. Mongoose simplifies interactions with MongoDB by providing a structured schema and powerful query capabilities.

Install Mongoose via npm:

```bash
npm install mongoose @types/mongoose
```

Mongoose also has excellent TypeScript support, so you'll be able to use types and interfaces for better type safety in your application.

Step 3: Connect to MongoDB

To connect your Node.js app to MongoDB using Mongoose, you need to establish a connection to the database. Create a file named db.ts for your MongoDB connection logic:

```typescript
import mongoose from 'mongoose';

const connectDB = async () => {
  try {
    await mongoose.connect('mongodb://localhost:27017/myapp', {
      useNewUrlParser: true,
      useUnifiedTopology: true,
    });
```

```
    console.log('MongoDB Connected');
  } catch (error) {
    console.error('Error connecting to MongoDB:',
error);
    process.exit(1);  // Exit the process with an
error code
  }
};


export default connectDB;
```

In this code, we are using `mongoose.connect` to connect to a local MongoDB instance (`mongodb://localhost:27017/myapp`). You can replace this URL with a MongoDB Atlas connection string if you're using the cloud service.

Now, call `connectDB()` in your main application file (`server.ts`):

typescript

```
import express from 'express';
import connectDB from './db';


const app = express();
const PORT = 3000;


connectDB();


app.listen(PORT, () => {
```

```
  console.log(`Server running on port ${PORT}`);
});
```

Designing Database Models and Schemas

In MongoDB, data is stored in **documents** within **collections**.
Mongoose allows you to define schemas to ensure that the data
structure is well-formed and consistent.

Creating a Product Model

For this section, let's design a simple product model that stores the
name, description, and price of a product.

Create a file called models/product.ts:

typescript

```
import mongoose, { Document, Schema } from
'mongoose';

interface IProduct extends Document {
  name: string;
  description: string;
  price: number;
}

const productSchema = new Schema<IProduct>({
```

```
  name: {
    type: String,
    required: true,
  },
  description: {
    type: String,
    required: true,
  },
  price: {
    type: Number,
    required: true,
  },
});


const Product = mongoose.model<IProduct>('Product',
productSchema);


export default Product;
```

Here, we:

- Define an interface `IProduct` that extends Mongoose's `Document` to include TypeScript types for the document fields.
- Create a `productSchema` with fields for `name`, `description`, and `price`.

- Use `mongoose.model()` to define the **Product** model that will be used to interact with the `products` collection in MongoDB.

Designing Database Relationships

While MongoDB is a NoSQL database and doesn't support traditional **foreign key constraints**, you can still model relationships between documents. This can be done using **references** or **embedded documents**.

For example, if you have a user and a product, you could store the product information directly in the user document (embedding) or use a reference to the product (referencing).

Reference Example (Using ObjectId)

In your `userSchema`, you can reference the `Product` model like this:

typescript

```
const userSchema = new Schema({
   name: String,
   email: String,
   purchasedProducts: [{ type:
mongoose.Schema.Types.ObjectId, ref: 'Product' }],
});
```

In this case, `purchasedProducts` is an array of references to `Product` documents. You can later populate this field with the actual product data using Mongoose's `.populate()` method.

Hands-On Project: Build a MongoDB Database with Mongoose for Your API

Step 1: Set Up the Express API to Handle Products

Now that you have a basic MongoDB connection and model set up, let's create the routes and logic to handle product operations in your API.

In `controllers/productController.ts`, create the CRUD operations:

```typescript
import { Request, Response } from 'express';
import Product from '../models/product';

export const getProducts = async (req: Request, res:
Response) => {
  try {
    const products = await Product.find();
    res.json(products);
  } catch (error) {
```

```
    res.status(500).json({ message: 'Error retrieving
products' });
  }
};


export const createProduct = async (req: Request,
res: Response) => {
  const { name, description, price } = req.body;

  try {
    const newProduct = new Product({ name,
description, price });
    await newProduct.save();
    res.status(201).json(newProduct);
  } catch (error) {
    res.status(500).json({ message: 'Error creating
product' });
  }
};
```

Step 2: Define Routes for CRUD Operations

In routes/productRoutes.ts, define the routes for product
operations:

```typescript
import { Router } from 'express';
import { getProducts, createProduct } from
'../controllers/productController';
```

```
const router = Router();

router.get('/products', getProducts);
router.post('/products', createProduct);

export default router;
```

Step 3: Integrate Routes into Express App

In your `server.ts`, use the `productRoutes`:

typescript

```typescript
import express from 'express';
import connectDB from './db';
import productRoutes from './routes/productRoutes';

const app = express();
app.use(express.json());

connectDB();

app.use('/api', productRoutes);

const PORT = 3000;
app.listen(PORT, () => {
  console.log(`Server running on port ${PORT}`);
});
```

Step 4: Testing the API

You can now test your API with a tool like Postman or Insomnia:

1. **GET /api/products**: Retrieve all products.
2. **POST /api/products**: Add a new product by sending a JSON body with `name`, `description`, and `price`.

Real-World Application: Understanding How Databases Power User Profiles in Apps

Databases play a vital role in modern applications, especially when it comes to **user profiles**. User profiles often contain personal information like names, email addresses, preferences, and past activities. Databases manage and store this information to enable features like authentication, authorization, and personalization.

For example, in a social media app like **Facebook**, MongoDB might store a user's profile data, including their posts, followers, and interactions. This data is then retrieved and used to display personalized content to the user.

MongoDB, with its flexibility and ability to handle large, unstructured data, is ideal for managing user-generated content and scaling as the number of users grows.

Chapter 8: Authentication and Authorization

What is Authentication and Why is it Important?

In modern web development, securing user data and ensuring that users are who they claim to be is critical. **Authentication** is the process of verifying the identity of a user, typically by requiring them to provide credentials such as a username and password. The goal of authentication is to confirm that the user is indeed who they say they are, before granting access to sensitive data or functionalities.

Why is Authentication Important?

Authentication is foundational to securing applications. Without proper authentication, anyone could potentially access a user's data or carry out actions on their behalf. It ensures that only authorized individuals can access specific resources within an application, protecting both user data and the integrity of the system.

Key reasons authentication is important include:

1. **Protecting Sensitive Data**: Authentication prevents unauthorized access to user data, such as personal information, payment details, and private messages.

2. **Maintaining Security**: It is essential to protect against identity theft, fraud, and unauthorized transactions.

3. **Personalization**: Authentication allows services to personalize experiences for the user, from showing custom content to maintaining a user's preferences.

4. **Regulatory Compliance**: Many industries have legal requirements for securely managing and protecting user data, such as HIPAA for healthcare or GDPR for the European Union.

In the next section, we'll explore **authorization**, which works alongside authentication to further protect applications by defining what authenticated users are allowed to do.

Authentication vs Authorization: Understanding the Difference

Although authentication and authorization are often used interchangeably, they are two distinct concepts in security.

Authentication

- **Definition**: Authentication is the process of confirming a user's identity. This is typically done using something the user knows (like a password), something the user has (like a phone or hardware token), or something the user is (like biometric data).

- **Goal**: The goal of authentication is to prove that the user is who they claim to be.

Authorization

- **Definition**: Authorization is the process of determining whether an authenticated user has permission to perform a specific action or access a particular resource. It is about defining what actions a user can or cannot perform.
- **Goal**: The goal of authorization is to ensure that users only have access to resources and actions they are permitted to interact with based on their roles or privileges.

To clarify, **authentication** is about verifying who you are, and **authorization** is about what you can do once you've been authenticated.

Implementing JWT Authentication in Node.js

One of the most common methods for implementing authentication in modern web applications is through **JSON Web Tokens (JWT)**. JWT is a compact, URL-safe token format that is used for securely transmitting information between parties. It's commonly used in stateless authentication systems, where the server doesn't store session data.

How JWT Authentication Works

JWT is used for **stateless authentication**—this means that the server does not store any session data between requests. Instead, the server issues a token when the user logs in, and the token contains information that can be used to verify the user's identity on subsequent requests.

A typical JWT consists of three parts:

1. **Header**: Contains metadata about the token, including the algorithm used to sign it.
2. **Payload**: Contains the claims, such as user information and token expiration.
3. **Signature**: Ensures that the token hasn't been tampered with.

Step 1: Install Required Packages

To implement JWT authentication in your Node.js app, you'll need the following dependencies:

- **jsonwebtoken**: A package to generate and verify JWTs.

- **bcryptjs:** A package to hash and compare passwords securely.

```bash
bash
```

```bash
npm install jsonwebtoken bcryptjs
```

Step 2: Create the JWT Authentication Logic

1. **Generate JWT Token:**

When the user logs in and provides valid credentials, you generate a JWT token. Here's how you can do it in your `authController.ts`:

```typescript
typescript
```

```typescript
import jwt from 'jsonwebtoken';
import bcrypt from 'bcryptjs';
import { Request, Response } from 'express';

const SECRET_KEY = 'your-secret-key';  // Store this
in environment variables

const loginUser = async (req: Request, res: Response)
=> {
  const { username, password } = req.body;

  // Find the user from the database
  const user = await User.findOne({ username });
```

```
  if (!user) {
    return res.status(400).json({ message: 'User not
found' });
  }

  // Compare the password
  const isMatch = await bcrypt.compare(password,
user.password);
  if (!isMatch) {
    return res.status(400).json({ message: 'Invalid
credentials' });
  }

  // Generate a JWT token
  const token = jwt.sign({ userId: user._id,
username: user.username }, SECRET_KEY, {
    expiresIn: '1h',  // Token expires in 1 hour
  });

  res.json({ token });
};

export { loginUser };
```

2. **Verify JWT Token:**

You'll need middleware to verify the token for routes that require authentication:

```typescript
import jwt from 'jsonwebtoken';
import { Request, Response, NextFunction } from
'express';

const SECRET_KEY = 'your-secret-key';

const authenticateJWT = (req: Request, res: Response,
next: NextFunction) => {
  const token =
req.header('Authorization')?.replace('Bearer ', '');

  if (!token) {
    return res.status(403).json({ message: 'Access
denied, no token provided' });
  }

  try {
    const decoded = jwt.verify(token, SECRET_KEY);
    req.user = decoded;
    next();  // Call the next middleware or route
handler
  } catch (error) {
    res.status(400).json({ message: 'Invalid token'
});
  }
};
```

```
export { authenticateJWT };
```

In the `authenticateJWT` middleware:

- The token is extracted from the `Authorization` header.
- The token is verified using the `jsonwebtoken.verify()` method. If the token is valid, the user's information is added to the request object (`req.user`), and the request continues.

Role-Based Access Control (RBAC)

Role-Based Access Control (RBAC) is a method of restricting access to a system based on the roles of individual users within an organization. RBAC ensures that users can only perform actions that are appropriate for their role.

How RBAC Works

In an RBAC system:

- **Roles**: Roles define the permissions assigned to a user (e.g., "admin," "user," "editor").
- **Permissions**: Permissions are actions that users can perform (e.g., "create," "edit," "delete").

- **Users**: Users are assigned roles, and each role has certain permissions.

For example:

- An **admin** can create, edit, delete, and view posts.
- A **user** can only view posts and create new ones.

Step 1: Assign Roles in the Database

In your **User** model, you can add a `role` field to assign roles to each user:

typescript

```typescript
const userSchema = new Schema({
  username: String,
  password: String,
  role: {
    type: String,
    enum: ['user', 'admin'],  // Restrict roles to
"user" or "admin"
    default: 'user',
  },
});
```

Step 2: Check User Roles

To manage user access based on roles, create middleware to check the user's role before allowing access to certain routes:

typescript

```typescript
const checkRole = (role: string) => {
  return (req: Request, res: Response, next:
NextFunction) => {
    if (req.user.role !== role) {
      return res.status(403).json({ message: 'Access
denied' });
    }
    next();
  };
};

export { checkRole };
```

You can use the checkRole middleware to restrict access to specific routes:

typescript

```typescript
app.get('/admin', authenticateJWT,
checkRole('admin'), (req, res) => {
  res.send('Welcome to the admin panel');
});
```

In this example:

- **authenticateJWT** ensures the user is authenticated.
- **checkRole('admin')** checks that the user has the "admin" role before allowing access to the route.

Hands-On Project: Implement JWT Authentication in Your Full-Stack App

In this hands-on project, you will implement JWT authentication in your full-stack application. The frontend will allow users to log in, and the backend will authenticate them, issue a JWT token, and return it to the frontend.

Step 1: Set Up Login Form in React

Create a simple login form where users can input their username and password. Upon submission, the form will send a request to the backend to authenticate the user.

```tsx
import React, { useState } from 'react';
import axios from 'axios';

const LoginForm: React.FC = () => {
```

```
  const [username, setUsername] = useState('');
  const [password, setPassword] = useState('');

  const handleSubmit = async (e: React.FormEvent) =>
{
    e.preventDefault();
    try {
      const response = await
axios.post('http://localhost:3000/api/login', {
username, password });
      localStorage.setItem('token',
response.data.token);
    } catch (error) {
      console.error('Login failed', error);
    }
  };

  return (
    <form onSubmit={handleSubmit}>
      <input type="text" placeholder="Username"
value={username} onChange={(e) =>
setUsername(e.target.value)} />
      <input type="password" placeholder="Password"
value={password} onChange={(e) =>
setPassword(e.target.value)} />
      <button type="submit">Login</button>
    </form>
  );
};
```

```
export default LoginForm;
```

Step 2: Handle Authentication on the Backend

In your backend, you will create a POST /api/login route to authenticate the user and issue a JWT token:

typescript

```typescript
import express from 'express';
import jwt from 'jsonwebtoken';
import bcrypt from 'bcryptjs';
import User from './models/user';

const app = express();
const SECRET_KEY = 'your-secret-key';

app.post('/api/login', async (req, res) => {
  const { username, password } = req.body;
  const user = await User.findOne({ username });

  if (!user) return res.status(400).json({ message:
'User not found' });

  const isMatch = await bcrypt.compare(password,
user.password);
  if (!isMatch) return res.status(400).json({
message: 'Invalid credentials' });
```

```
  const token = jwt.sign({ userId: user._id,
username: user.username, role: user.role },
SECRET_KEY, { expiresIn: '1h' });
  res.json({ token });
});

app.listen(3000, () => console.log('Server running on
port 3000'));
```

This route verifies the user's credentials and generates a JWT token that is returned to the frontend. The frontend can store this token (e.g., in `localStorage`) and use it to authenticate subsequent requests.

Real-World Application: How User Authentication Works in a SaaS Application

In **Software-as-a-Service (SaaS)** applications, user authentication plays a crucial role in providing access to resources, managing user roles, and ensuring data privacy. Here's how authentication and authorization are typically implemented in SaaS platforms:

1. **User Registration**: Users create an account by providing their credentials, which are stored securely in the database after hashing their passwords.

2. **User Login**: After registration, users log in using their credentials. The backend verifies the credentials and issues a JWT token, which is sent to the frontend.

3. **Role-Based Access Control (RBAC)**: The system assigns roles to users, such as "admin," "manager," or "customer." These roles dictate what actions and resources the user can access.

4. **Data Privacy**: In SaaS applications, it's essential to ensure that users can only access their data. JWT tokens, along with RBAC, are used to enforce this by verifying the user's identity and role before granting access to sensitive information.

For instance, in a project management SaaS platform, an **admin** user can access all projects, while a **regular user** can only access the projects they are part of. JWT tokens are used to authenticate users and check their roles before allowing access to specific project resources.

Chapter 9: Building Scalable Microservices with TypeScript

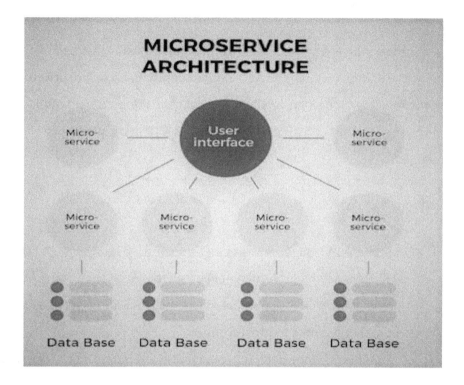

What are Microservices?

Introduction to Microservices Architecture

In traditional monolithic architectures, all components of an application—frontend, backend, and database—are bundled together into a single codebase. While this approach works well for small to medium-sized applications, it becomes difficult to scale and maintain as the application grows. The **microservices architecture** is a modern approach to building software that focuses on breaking down an application into smaller, independent services, each responsible for a specific piece of functionality.

A **microservice** is a self-contained unit of functionality that can be developed, deployed, and scaled independently. Each microservice is responsible for a single business domain and interacts with other microservices through APIs, typically using HTTP or messaging queues.

Advantages of Microservices

1. **Scalability**: Microservices can be scaled independently, allowing teams to allocate resources to the services that need it most. This is particularly useful when some services experience more load than others.
2. **Flexibility**: Since each microservice is a separate unit, you can use different technologies for different services. For example, you could have one service running on Node.js, another on Python, and yet another on Java, depending on the requirements of each service.
3. **Fault Isolation**: With microservices, a failure in one service doesn't necessarily mean the entire system goes down. Each

service is isolated, which means issues can be contained within a single service, improving overall system reliability.

4. **Faster Development**: Since microservices are small and independent, they can be developed by different teams in parallel. This reduces development time and makes it easier to implement new features and improvements.

5. **Continuous Deployment**: Microservices enable continuous integration and continuous deployment (CI/CD) because each service can be updated independently without affecting the entire system.

6. **Easier Maintenance**: With the application broken down into smaller pieces, it's easier to understand, maintain, and update each microservice independently. It's also easier to troubleshoot and resolve issues as you're only dealing with a small subset of the application.

Designing a Microservice with TypeScript and Node.js

In this section, we'll explore how to design and implement microservices using **TypeScript** and **Node.js**. TypeScript is a great choice for building microservices because it offers type safety, which can catch errors at compile-time, leading to fewer bugs and easier-to-maintain code.

Step 1: Setting Up the Project

To get started, create a new directory for your microservice and initialize the project:

```bash
mkdir inventory-microservice
cd inventory-microservice
npm init -y
npm install typescript express axios
npm install --save-dev @types/node @types/express
```

- **TypeScript**: Adds type safety to JavaScript, ensuring your code is more predictable and easier to debug.
- **Express**: A web framework for Node.js, commonly used to build REST APIs.
- **Axios**: A promise-based HTTP client for making requests from your microservices to other services.

Next, create a `tsconfig.json` file to configure TypeScript settings:

```bash
npx tsc --init
```

You can modify the `tsconfig.json` to specify where TypeScript should output compiled code:

```json
{
  "compilerOptions": {
    "target": "ES6",
    "module": "CommonJS",
    "outDir": "./dist",
    "strict": true,
    "esModuleInterop": true
  },
  "include": ["src/**/*.ts"]
}
```

Step 2: Design the Inventory Microservice

Let's assume this microservice is responsible for managing a store's inventory. It should be able to add products, update product details, and retrieve product information.

Modeling the Data

Create a file called `models/product.ts` to define the structure of your data:

```typescript
export interface Product {
  id: number;
  name: string;
```

```
  description: string;
  quantity: number;
  price: number;
}
```

Creating the Service

Now, let's create a simple API to handle product operations. Create `src/server.ts`:

typescript

```typescript
import express, { Request, Response } from 'express';
import { Product } from './models/product';

const app = express();
app.use(express.json());

let products: Product[] = [];

app.get('/products', (req: Request, res: Response) =>
{
  res.json(products);
});

app.post('/products', (req: Request, res: Response)
=> {
  const { name, description, quantity, price }:
Product = req.body;
  const newProduct: Product = {
```

```
    id: products.length + 1,
    name,
    description,
    quantity,
    price,
  };
  products.push(newProduct);
  res.status(201).json(newProduct);
});

app.put('/products/:id', (req: Request, res:
Response) => {
  const { id } = req.params;
  const { name, description, quantity, price }:
Product = req.body;

  const productIndex = products.findIndex((product)
=> product.id === parseInt(id));
  if (productIndex === -1) {
    return res.status(404).json({ message: 'Product
not found' });
  }

  products[productIndex] = { id: parseInt(id), name,
description, quantity, price };
  res.json(products[productIndex]);
});
```

```
app.delete('/products/:id', (req: Request, res:
Response) => {
  const { id } = req.params;
  products = products.filter((product) => product.id
!== parseInt(id));
  res.status(204).send();
});

const PORT = 3000;
app.listen(PORT, () => {
  console.log(`Inventory service is running on
http://localhost:${PORT}`);
});
```

Here's what's happening in the code:

- **GET /products**: Retrieves all products in the inventory.
- **POST /products**: Adds a new product to the inventory.
- **PUT /products/:id**: Updates an existing product's details.
- **DELETE /products/:id**: Removes a product from the inventory.

Step 3: Run the Service

Compile the TypeScript code and start the service:

```
bash
```

```
npx tsc
```

```
node dist/server.js
```

Your inventory microservice should now be running and accessible at `http://localhost:3000`.

Service Discovery and Load Balancing

As your system grows and you add more microservices, managing multiple services becomes increasingly complex. Two key concepts for ensuring your microservices communicate efficiently are **service discovery** and **load balancing**.

What is Service Discovery?

Service discovery refers to the process of automatically detecting and connecting to services in a distributed system. In a microservices architecture, services are dynamic, meaning they can be added, removed, or moved across different servers or containers. Service discovery tools help manage this complexity by allowing services to locate and communicate with each other without needing hardcoded IP addresses.

- **Tools for Service Discovery**:
    - **Consul**: A popular tool for service discovery and health checking.

- o **Eureka**: A service discovery platform used by Netflix.
- o **Kubernetes**: When using container orchestration with Kubernetes, it provides built-in service discovery.

What is Load Balancing?

Load balancing is the process of distributing network traffic across multiple servers to ensure no single server becomes overwhelmed. This is crucial for maintaining performance and availability, especially when dealing with large-scale systems.

- **Types of Load Balancing**:
  - o **Round-robin**: Distributes requests equally across all services.
  - o **Least connections**: Routes traffic to the service with the least number of active connections.
  - o **Weighted load balancing**: Routes more traffic to more powerful services.

Tools like **NGINX** or **HAProxy** can help balance traffic between multiple instances of a service.

Hands-On Project: Build a Simple Inventory Microservice with TypeScript

Now that we've set up a basic inventory service, let's enhance it by implementing **service discovery** and **load balancing**.

Step 1: Add Service Discovery with Consul

1. Install and run **Consul** on your local machine or use a cloud provider like AWS.
2. Register your inventory microservice with Consul by adding health checks and the service definition to a configuration file.

For example, create a `consul-register.json` file:

json

```json
{
  "service": {
    "name": "inventory-service",
    "tags": ["node"],
    "port": 3000,
    "check": {
      "http": "http://localhost:3000/health",
      "interval": "10s"
    }
  }
}
```

```
}
```

Run Consul to register your service:

```
bash
```

```
consul agent -dev
consul services register consul-register.json
```

Step 2: Implement Load Balancing with NGINX

1. Install **NGINX** on your machine.

2. Create an `nginx.conf` file to define load balancing rules:

```
nginx
```

```nginx
http {
    upstream inventory-service {
        server localhost:3000;
        server localhost:3001;
    }

    server {
        location / {
            proxy_pass http://inventory-service;
        }
    }
}
```

This configuration will route traffic to multiple instances of the inventory service. You can now run multiple instances of your inventory microservice, and NGINX will balance the load.

Real-World Application: How Microservices Are Used in the Logistics Industry for Tracking Shipments

In industries like logistics, microservices are used to break down complex systems into manageable, independent units. A typical logistics platform might consist of several microservices responsible for different aspects of the business:

1. **Shipment Tracking**: One microservice might be responsible for managing the shipment process, including tracking locations, shipping routes, and delivery statuses.
2. **Inventory Management**: Another microservice could handle the inventory of goods, ensuring that products are in stock and available for shipment.
3. **Payment Processing**: A payment microservice would securely handle transactions, billing, and invoicing.
4. **User Management**: A microservice for managing user accounts, authentication, and roles.

These services communicate with each other through well-defined APIs and are often coordinated by a central system that ensures the flow of information between services. For example, when a package is shipped, the **shipment tracking microservice** communicates with the **inventory microservice** to update stock levels, and with the **payment service** to ensure the transaction is complete.

Chapter 10: Real-Time Applications with WebSockets

Introduction to WebSockets

What is WebSocket and How It Enables Real-Time Communication?

In modern web applications, providing **real-time communication** is crucial for enhancing user engagement and creating interactive experiences. Whether it's for instant messaging, live notifications, or interactive games, the ability to push updates from the server to the client instantly is a core feature in today's dynamic apps.

WebSocket is a **communication protocol** that enables **two-way, full-duplex communication** between the client (browser) and the server over a single, long-lived connection. Unlike traditional HTTP requests, where the client sends a request to the server and waits for a response, WebSocket allows the server to send data to the client at any time. This provides a highly efficient, real-time communication channel between both parties.

Here's a breakdown of key concepts regarding WebSockets:

- **Full-Duplex Communication**: WebSocket creates a two-way communication channel that allows both the server and the client to send and receive data simultaneously.
- **Persistent Connection**: Once the WebSocket connection is established, it remains open, allowing continuous data transfer without the need to reopen the connection for each exchange.
- **Low Latency**: WebSocket provides lower latency compared to traditional HTTP requests because data is transferred immediately as it becomes available, without waiting for the next request from the client.
- **Use Cases**: Real-time messaging (e.g., chat apps), live sports scores, financial market updates, and collaborative tools (e.g., Google Docs).

In contrast to HTTP, which is **request-response** based (meaning the client sends a request and waits for a response), WebSocket is **event-driven**, allowing data to flow both ways without needing to wait for a request.

How WebSocket Works

WebSocket works by upgrading an HTTP connection to a WebSocket connection. Here's how the WebSocket connection is established:

1. The client sends an **HTTP request** to the server to initiate a WebSocket connection (using a `GET` request with the `Upgrade: websocket` header).
2. The server acknowledges the request and **upgrade the connection** from HTTP to WebSocket.
3. Once the WebSocket connection is established, both the client and the server can send and receive data over the same connection without the need to re-establish a connection.

Implementing WebSockets in Node.js with TypeScript

Setting Up a WebSocket Server in Node.js

Node.js is an ideal platform for building WebSocket-based real-time applications because of its event-driven, non-blocking I/O model. To implement WebSockets in Node.js, we can use the **ws** library, which provides an easy-to-use API for WebSocket communication.

Step 1: Install Dependencies

First, let's set up a simple Node.js server with TypeScript and install the required dependencies.

bash

```
npm init -y
```

```
npm install ws express typescript @types/node
@types/express @types/ws
```

- **ws**: The WebSocket library for creating a WebSocket server.
- **express**: The web framework to create an HTTP server.
- **typescript**: The TypeScript compiler.
- **@types/***: TypeScript type definitions for the libraries.

Step 2: Set Up TypeScript Configuration

Create a `tsconfig.json` file for TypeScript:

bash

```
npx tsc --init
```

Here's an example of a basic `tsconfig.json`:

json

```
{
  "compilerOptions": {
    "target": "ES6",
    "module": "CommonJS",
    "strict": true,
    "esModuleInterop": true,
    "outDir": "./dist"
  },
  "include": ["src/**/*.ts"]
```

```
}
```

Step 3: Create a WebSocket Server

Now, let's create a WebSocket server using the `ws` library. Create a `src/server.ts` file:

typescript

```typescript
import express from 'express';
import WebSocket, { Server } from 'ws';

const app = express();
const PORT = 3000;

// Set up HTTP server
const server = app.listen(PORT, () => {
  console.log(`Server running on
http://localhost:${PORT}`);
});

// Set up WebSocket server on top of HTTP server
const wss = new Server({ server });

wss.on('connection', (ws) => {
  console.log('A new client connected');

  // Send a welcome message to the client
  ws.send('Welcome to the WebSocket server!');
```

```
// Listen for messages from the client
ws.on('message', (message) => {
  console.log('Received message:', message);
  // Broadcast the message to all connected clients
  wss.clients.forEach((client) => {
    if (client !== ws && client.readyState ===
WebSocket.OPEN) {
      client.send(message.toString());
    }
  });
});

// Handle connection close
ws.on('close', () => {
  console.log('A client disconnected');
});
});
```

In this example:

- **WebSocket server**: We create a WebSocket server using the
  ws library, which listens for incoming WebSocket
  connections.
- **Message handling**: The server sends a welcome message
  when a client connects and listens for incoming messages
  from the client. When a message is received, it broadcasts
  the message to all connected clients except the sender.

Step 4: Run the WebSocket Server

Compile the TypeScript code and run the WebSocket server:

bash

```
npx tsc
node dist/server.js
```

Your WebSocket server is now running and ready to accept connections from WebSocket clients.

Handling Real-Time Data in React

Integrating WebSockets with React

Now that the WebSocket server is set up, let's focus on how to connect React to the WebSocket server and handle real-time data. In this section, we'll create a simple chat application where users can send messages and receive updates in real-time.

Step 1: Create a WebSocket Client in React

To connect to the WebSocket server, we'll use the **WebSocket API** available in modern browsers.

Create a new React component called `Chat.tsx`:

```tsx
import React, { useState, useEffect } from 'react';

const Chat: React.FC = () => {
  const [messages, setMessages] =
useState<string[]>([]);
  const [input, setInput] = useState('');
  const [socket, setSocket] = useState<WebSocket |
null>(null);

  useEffect(() => {
    const ws = new WebSocket('ws://localhost:3000');

    ws.onopen = () => {
      console.log('Connected to WebSocket server');
    };

    ws.onmessage = (event) => {
      setMessages((prevMessages) => [...prevMessages,
event.data]);
    };

    ws.onclose = () => {
      console.log('Disconnected from WebSocket
server');
    };

    setSocket(ws);
```

```
  // Cleanup on component unmount
  return () => {
    ws.close();
  };
}, []);


const sendMessage = () => {
  if (socket && input.trim()) {
    socket.send(input);
    setInput('');
  }
};


return (
  <div>
    <h2>Chat Room</h2>
    <div>
      <ul>
        {messages.map((message, index) => (
          <li key={index}>{message}</li>
        ))}
      </ul>
    </div>
    <input
      type="text"
      value={input}
      onChange={(e) => setInput(e.target.value)}
      placeholder="Type a message..."
```

```
      />
      <button onClick={sendMessage}>Send</button>
    </div>
  );
};
```

```
export default Chat;
```

Step 2: Add WebSocket to Your Application

Now, you can use the Chat component in your App.tsx:

tsx

```
import React from 'react';
import Chat from './Chat';

const App: React.FC = () => {
  return (
    <div>
      <Chat />
    </div>
  );
};
```

```
export default App;
```

In this code:

- **WebSocket connection**: We establish a WebSocket connection in the `useEffect` hook when the component is mounted and clean it up when the component is unmounted.
- **Handling messages**: Incoming messages are appended to the `messages` state, which is rendered in the UI as a list.
- **Sending messages**: The `sendMessage` function sends the input text to the WebSocket server when the user clicks the "Send" button.

Hands-On Project: Build a Simple Chat Application with Node.js, WebSockets, and React

Let's bring everything together by building a complete real-time chat application.

Step 1: Set Up WebSocket Server (Node.js)

Use the `ws` library, as shown in the previous section, to create a WebSocket server. This server will handle incoming WebSocket connections and broadcast messages to all clients.

Step 2: Create Chat UI (React)

In the `Chat.tsx` component, users can type messages, which will be sent to the WebSocket server, and received messages will be displayed in real-time.

Step 3: Connect Frontend and Backend

Run the WebSocket server and the React frontend on different ports (React on `3000`, WebSocket server on `3001`). The React app will connect to the WebSocket server at `ws://localhost:3001`.

Step 4: Run the Application

1. Start the WebSocket server (`node dist/server.js`).
2. Start the React development server (`npm start`).
3. Open multiple browser tabs and send messages in real-time between them.

Real-World Application: How Real-Time Applications Work in Customer Support Tools

In real-world applications like **customer support tools**, WebSockets are often used to facilitate real-time communication between customers and support agents. Here's how it works:

1. **Live Chat**: Customer support tools often include live chat functionality where customers can ask questions, and support agents respond in real-time. WebSockets provide the instant data transfer necessary for these interactions to happen smoothly.

2. **Notifications**: Support agents are notified immediately when new tickets are created or when there is an update on an existing ticket, allowing them to respond quickly.

3. **Collaborative Features**: Support agents often collaborate on the same tickets. With WebSockets, they can see real-time updates, comments, or status changes made by other agents, ensuring everyone is on the same page.

4. **Ticket Updates**: As a customer or agent updates the status of a support ticket (e.g., moving it from "open" to "closed"), WebSockets ensure all parties (agents, customers) are immediately notified of the change.

By using WebSockets, customer support tools can reduce response time, improve collaboration among agents, and create a more engaging experience for users.

Chapter 11: Testing and Debugging Your Full-Stack App

The Importance of Testing in Software Development

Why Testing is Crucial

Testing is a fundamental part of software development that helps ensure your application works as expected. It involves writing tests that check if individual parts of your application are functioning correctly. The goal of testing is to catch bugs early in the development process, provide confidence that your code works as intended, and ultimately ensure that your users receive a reliable product.

The key reasons testing is important are:

1. **Quality Assurance**: Testing ensures that your application behaves as expected and meets the requirements. It helps prevent defects from being introduced into the codebase and ensures that bugs are caught before they affect users.
2. **Faster Development**: Although writing tests can initially slow down development, it ultimately speeds up the development process. Developers can confidently make

changes to the codebase knowing that the tests will catch any unintended side effects.

3. **Refactoring Confidence**: Over time, your application's code will change as you add new features and improve existing ones. Tests ensure that refactoring doesn't break the functionality of the system.

4. **Collaboration and Communication**: Tests act as documentation for other developers working on the project. They provide clear expectations of how the application should behave, improving communication across the development team.

5. **Preventing Regression**: As your application evolves, regression testing ensures that new features don't introduce old bugs. It helps maintain the integrity of your app over time.

Types of Tests

There are different types of tests used in software development, each focusing on different levels of the application:

- **Unit Tests**: Unit tests focus on testing individual pieces of functionality, typically functions or components, in isolation from the rest of the system. These tests verify that a function or method behaves correctly given a specific input.

- **Integration Tests**: Integration tests check how multiple components of your application work together. These tests are important for ensuring that different parts of your system interact correctly with each other.
- **End-to-End (E2E) Tests**: E2E tests simulate user interactions with the application, testing the system as a whole to ensure it behaves correctly from the user's perspective.

Introduction to Testing Frameworks like Mocha, Jest, and Chai

Testing frameworks are tools that help you write and run tests in a structured and organized way. They provide methods for writing assertions, organizing tests, and running them automatically. Some popular testing frameworks for full-stack JavaScript development include **Mocha, Jest**, and **Chai**.

Mocha

Mocha is a flexible and feature-rich JavaScript test framework running on **Node.js**. It provides a simple interface to write and run tests and supports multiple assertion libraries like Chai.

- **Pros**: Highly customizable and works well with other libraries.
- **Cons**: Needs additional libraries (like Chai) for assertions and spies.

Jest

Jest is a popular JavaScript testing framework developed by Facebook, mainly used for testing React applications, but it works well with both frontend and backend applications. Jest comes with a built-in assertion library, mocking capabilities, and supports snapshot testing, making it an excellent all-in-one solution for testing.

- **Pros**: Easy to set up, built-in assertion library, great for testing React components.
- **Cons**: May be overkill for simpler projects.

Chai

Chai is an assertion library often used in conjunction with Mocha. It provides a variety of assertion styles, including **TDD (Test-Driven Development)** and **BDD (Behavior-Driven Development)**, making it easy to write readable and expressive tests.

- **Pros**: Flexible assertion styles, can be used with other frameworks.
- **Cons**: Requires an additional setup with Mocha.

For most full-stack applications, **Jest** is recommended due to its simplicity and built-in features, especially when working with React. **Mocha** and **Chai** are often preferred in more complex setups or when you need more customization.

Unit Testing with Jest

Unit testing is the practice of testing individual functions, methods, or components in isolation to ensure they behave as expected. With Jest, you can easily write and execute unit tests in your Node.js and React applications.

Setting Up Jest

1. **Install Jest** in your project:

    bash

    ```
    npm install --save-dev jest @types/jest ts-jest
    ```

2. **Configure Jest for TypeScript** by adding a `jest.config.js` file:

```js
js
```

```js
module.exports = {
  preset: 'ts-jest',
  testEnvironment: 'node',
};
```

3. **Add a test script** in `package.json` to run Jest:

```json
json
```

```json
"scripts": {
  "test": "jest"
}
```

Writing Unit Tests for React Components

In your React components, you may want to test individual methods or the component's behavior in different states. For example, you can test a simple button component:

```tsx
tsx
```

```tsx
// Button.tsx
import React from 'react';

interface ButtonProps {
  label: string;
  onClick: () => void;
}
```

```
const Button: React.FC<ButtonProps> = ({ label,
onClick }) => (
    <button onClick={onClick}>{label}</button>
);
```

```
export default Button;
```

Now, let's write a unit test for this component in `Button.test.tsx`:

tsx

```
import { render, screen, fireEvent } from '@testing-
library/react';
import Button from './Button';
```

```
test('renders button with label and handles click',
() => {
    const handleClick = jest.fn();

    render(<Button label="Click Me"
onClick={handleClick} />);

    const button = screen.getByText('Click Me');
    fireEvent.click(button);

    expect(handleClick).toHaveBeenCalledTimes(1);
});
```

This test does two things:

1. It renders the `Button` component with a label and a mock click handler.
2. It simulates a click event and verifies that the click handler is called exactly once.

Writing Unit Tests for Node.js API

For testing your Node.js API, Jest can be used to mock database calls and test API routes. Here's an example of testing a simple API endpoint that retrieves a list of products:

typescript

```typescript
import request from 'supertest';
import app from './server'; // Assume you have an
Express app

describe('GET /products', () => {
  it('should return a list of products', async () =>
{
    const response = await
request(app).get('/products');

    expect(response.status).toBe(200);
    expect(response.body).toHaveLength(3); //
Assuming there are 3 products in the mock data
```

```
    });
});
```

Here, `supertest` is used to send HTTP requests to the API, and Jest's `expect` function is used for assertions.

Integration and End-to-End Testing

What is Integration Testing?

Integration testing is the practice of testing how multiple parts of your application interact. It checks whether the components work together as expected. In a full-stack application, integration tests might involve testing the interaction between your React frontend and Node.js backend, ensuring that data flows correctly between the two.

For example, an integration test might verify that the frontend correctly displays data fetched from the backend API. In this case, you would set up a test environment where both the backend and frontend are running, and then simulate a full transaction (e.g., making an API request from React and checking the data in the UI).

What is End-to-End (E2E) Testing?

End-to-end testing simulates a user interacting with your entire application, from the frontend to the backend, to ensure that the system works as a whole. E2E testing is usually done with tools like **Cypress** or **Selenium**, and it allows you to test user interactions, such as logging in, navigating between pages, and submitting forms.

Setting Up Cypress for End-to-End Testing

Cypress is a popular tool for end-to-end testing in modern web applications. It provides an easy-to-use interface and is designed to work seamlessly with both React and Node.js.

Step 1: Install Cypress

To get started with Cypress, install it as a development dependency:

bash

```
npm install --save-dev cypress
```

Step 2: Set Up Cypress Configuration

Once installed, you can open Cypress for the first time by running:

bash

```
npx cypress open
```

This will open the Cypress test runner, where you can create your tests. The tests are typically stored in the `cypress/integration` directory.

Step 3: Writing End-to-End Tests

Create an E2E test for your chat application:

js

```js
describe('Chat App', () => {
  it('should send and receive messages', () => {
    cy.visit('http://localhost:3000');

    cy.get('input[type="text"]').type('Hello, World!');
    cy.get('button').click();

    cy.get('ul').should('contain', 'Hello, World!');
  });
});
```

This test simulates typing a message into the input field, clicking the send button, and verifying that the message appears in the list.

Hands-On Project: Write Unit Tests for Your Full-Stack App

In this project, you will write unit tests for both your React frontend and Node.js backend to ensure your full-stack application is working correctly.

Step 1: Unit Tests for React Components

Write unit tests for the components in your full-stack app, such as login forms, chat interfaces, and product listings. Use Jest with **React Testing Library** to test the components.

Step 2: Unit Tests for Node.js API

Write tests for your API routes to check that they return the expected responses. Use **supertest** to send HTTP requests to your API and assert the correct responses.

Step 3: Integration Tests

Write integration tests to check that the frontend and backend work together. For example, you might test that the React app correctly renders data fetched from the Node.js API.

Step 4: End-to-End Tests

Write E2E tests with Cypress to simulate user interactions with your full-stack app. Verify that the entire user journey (e.g., logging in, viewing products, submitting forms) works as expected.

Real-World Application: How Testing Ensures Reliability in Financial Applications

In **financial applications**, testing is critical due to the sensitivity of the data and the need for high reliability. Here's how testing ensures reliability in this domain:

1. **Data Accuracy**: Financial applications need to calculate and display accurate data, such as balances, transactions, and investments. Testing ensures that the math behind these calculations is correct.
2. **Security**: Financial apps deal with personal and sensitive data. Tests are used to check for vulnerabilities like **SQL injection, cross-site scripting (XSS)**, and **data leaks**.
3. **Transaction Integrity**: Testing ensures that transactions (e.g., transfers, withdrawals, deposits) are processed correctly and consistently, with proper validation and handling of edge cases like insufficient funds.

4. **Regulatory Compliance**: Financial apps must comply with legal standards like **PCI-DSS** (Payment Card Industry Data Security Standard) and **GDPR** (General Data Protection Regulation). Testing ensures that the app meets these regulations.

Testing in financial applications reduces the risk of errors that could result in financial loss, data breaches, or legal issues. Rigorous testing ensures that the system functions properly under normal conditions and handles edge cases appropriately.

Chapter 12: Deploying Full-Stack JavaScript Applications

Introduction to Deployment

What is Deployment, and Why is it Important?

Deployment refers to the process of moving your application from the local development environment to a production environment, where users can access it. It involves making sure that your app is live, accessible via the internet, and performs reliably. Deployment isn't just about hosting your application; it also involves ensuring that the app functions well in production, can handle user traffic, and is free of bugs that might have been overlooked during development.

The importance of deployment can be summed up in several points:

1. **Access and Accessibility**: Deployment is crucial because it enables users to access your application. Without deployment, your app would only exist locally on your machine and would not be available to the public.

2. **Reliability**: A successful deployment ensures that your app works in real-world conditions, handling various user interactions and scaling as needed. It's vital to monitor the

app's behavior once it's live to ensure everything functions smoothly.

3. **User Experience**: Proper deployment affects the user experience. It ensures that your application is fast, responsive, and can handle multiple users without crashing.

4. **Updates and Maintenance**: Deployment also includes the ability to roll out updates and patches. Continuous deployment tools help keep the app up-to-date with minimal downtime.

Deploying a Node.js App with Heroku

Heroku is one of the easiest cloud platforms to deploy Node.js applications to. It abstracts much of the complexity involved in setting up a server and allows developers to focus on writing their code rather than managing infrastructure.

Step 1: Setting Up Heroku

To get started, you'll need to install the **Heroku CLI** (Command Line Interface) on your machine. The Heroku CLI lets you interact with your Heroku apps directly from the command line.

1. **Install Heroku CLI**: Download the installer for your operating system from Heroku's website and follow the instructions.

2. **Log in to Heroku**: After installation, log in to your Heroku account by running:

bash

```
heroku login
```

This will open a browser window asking for your Heroku credentials.

Step 2: Prepare Your Node.js Application for Deployment

Before you can deploy, make sure your Node.js application is ready for deployment. A few things you need to check:

1. `Procfile`: Heroku uses a `Procfile` to determine how to run your application. In the root directory of your app, create a `Procfile` with the following content:

bash

```
web: node dist/server.js
```

This tells Heroku to run the `server.js` file using Node.js.

2. **Ensure the `package.json` is Set Up**: Your `package.json` file should include the necessary dependencies and scripts for production. Here's an example:

json

```json
{
  "name": "my-node-app",
  "version": "1.0.0",
  "main": "server.js",
  "dependencies": {
    "express": "^4.17.1",
    "mongoose": "^5.9.7"
  },
  "scripts": {
    "start": "node dist/server.js",
    "dev": "nodemon src/server.ts"
  },
  "engines": {
    "node": "14.x"
  }
}
```

3. **Build and Compile**: Since you're using TypeScript, you'll
   need to build your app before deployment. You can do this by
   running:

bash

```bash
npx tsc
```

This will compile your TypeScript files into JavaScript and output them into the `dist/` directory (as specified in the `tsconfig.json`).

Step 3: Deploy to Heroku

1. **Create a Heroku Application**: To create a new app on Heroku, run:

   bash

   ```
   heroku create my-node-app
   ```

   This command creates a new app with a unique URL (e.g., `my-node-app.herokuapp.com`).

2. **Add Your Code to Git**: Heroku uses Git to deploy applications. Initialize a Git repository if you haven't already:

   bash

   ```
   git init
   git add .
   git commit -m "Initial commit"
   ```

3. **Deploy to Heroku**: Now, deploy your app by pushing your code to Heroku's Git remote:

```bash
git push heroku master
```

4. **Open Your App**: Once the deployment is complete, open your app in the browser:

```bash
heroku open
```

Your Node.js app is now live!

Deploying a React App with Netlify

Netlify is a popular platform for deploying frontend applications, especially those built with React. It offers continuous deployment out of the box, making it easy to host your static assets.

Step 1: Setting Up Netlify

1. **Create a Netlify Account**: Go to Netlify's website and sign up for a free account.
2. **Install Netlify CLI** (optional for local testing):

```bash
```

```
npm install -g netlify-cli
```

Step 2: Build the React Application for Production

To deploy your React app to Netlify, first, you need to build it for production. Run the following command to create a production-ready build:

```bash
```

```
npm run build
```

This will generate a build/ folder containing the optimized, static files for your React app.

Step 3: Deploy to Netlify

1. **Create a New Site**: In your Netlify dashboard, click on the "New site from Git" button and connect your Git repository (e.g., GitHub, GitLab, or Bitbucket).

2. **Set the Build Command**: During the setup process, set the build command to npm run build and the publish directory to build/ (the default for React apps).

3. **Deploy**: Netlify will automatically deploy your app every time you push to the connected Git repository. It will also provide you with a unique URL to view your deployed React app.

Step 4: Link to Your Backend

To connect your React app to the backend (Node.js app) deployed on Heroku, ensure that your React app makes HTTP requests to the correct backend URL (Heroku app URL).

CI/CD Pipeline for Automated Deployments

What is CI/CD?

CI (Continuous Integration) and **CD (Continuous Deployment)** are key practices in modern software development that allow for automating the process of testing and deploying applications. CI/CD pipelines streamline and automate the process of integrating code changes and deploying them to production.

- **Continuous Integration (CI)**: CI refers to the practice of automatically testing and merging code changes into the main branch (typically using tools like GitHub Actions or Jenkins). This ensures that new code integrates smoothly with the existing codebase and doesn't break existing features.
- **Continuous Deployment (CD)**: CD is the process of automatically deploying new changes to production after passing CI tests. It eliminates the need for manual

deployment, reducing the chance of human error and speeding up the release process.

Step 1: Setting Up GitHub Actions

GitHub Actions is a powerful automation tool integrated directly into GitHub repositories. It enables you to create workflows that automate CI/CD tasks.

1. **Create a Workflow File:** In your GitHub repository, create a `.github/workflows` directory and add a file named `deploy.yml`.
2. **Define the Workflow:**

Here's an example of a simple GitHub Actions workflow for deploying your full-stack app to Heroku and Netlify:

```yaml
name: Full-Stack App Deployment

on:
  push:
    branches:
      - master

jobs:
  deploy:
```

```yaml
    runs-on: ubuntu-latest
    steps:
      # Checkout code from repository
      - name: Checkout code
        uses: actions/checkout@v2

      # Set up Node.js for backend deployment
      - name: Set up Node.js
        uses: actions/setup-node@v2
        with:
          node-version: '14'

      # Install dependencies for backend
      - name: Install backend dependencies
        run: |
          cd backend
          npm install

      # Deploy backend to Heroku
      - name: Deploy backend to Heroku
        run: |
          git remote add heroku
https://git.heroku.com/your-app-name.git
          git push heroku master
        env:
          HEROKU_API_KEY: ${{ secrets.HEROKU_API_KEY
}}

      # Install dependencies for frontend
```

```
    - name: Install frontend dependencies
      run: |
        cd frontend
        npm install

    # Deploy frontend to Netlify
    - name: Deploy frontend to Netlify
      run: |
        npm run build
        netlify deploy --prod --dir=frontend/build
      env:
        NETLIFY_AUTH_TOKEN: ${{
secrets.NETLIFY_AUTH_TOKEN }}
```

In this workflow:

- The pipeline runs when there's a push to the `master` branch.
- It installs dependencies for both the backend (Node.js) and frontend (React).
- Deploys the backend to Heroku and the frontend to Netlify.

Step 2: Configure Secrets

In your GitHub repository, go to **Settings > Secrets** and add your Heroku API key and Netlify authentication token to securely store your credentials.

Hands-On Project: Deploy a Full-Stack Application to the Cloud

In this project, we will deploy a full-stack JavaScript application with a **Node.js backend** on **Heroku** and a **React frontend** on **Netlify**. The application could be a simple inventory management system where users can add, update, and delete products.

Step 1: Deploy the Backend (Node.js) to Heroku

- Set up your Node.js app and ensure it's production-ready.
- Follow the steps in the "Deploying a Node.js App with Heroku" section to push the app to Heroku.

Step 2: Deploy the Frontend (React) to Netlify

- Ensure your React app is production-ready with `npm run build`.
- Follow the steps in the "Deploying a React App with Netlify" section to deploy the frontend.

Step 3: Implement Continuous Deployment

- Set up GitHub Actions to automate the deployment process as described in the "CI/CD Pipeline for Automated Deployments" section.

Once your app is deployed, make sure everything works by testing both the frontend and backend.

Real-World Application: Understanding How GitHub Actions and CI/CD Pipelines Work in Production

In real-world production environments, **CI/CD pipelines** are integral to modern software development. GitHub Actions, Jenkins, CircleCI, and other CI/CD tools automate the deployment of new features, bug fixes, and updates.

Here's how it works in a production environment:

1. **Automated Testing**: Before deploying to production, CI tools run unit, integration, and end-to-end tests to ensure new changes don't break the application.
2. **Deployment to Staging**: Changes are first deployed to a staging environment where additional tests are performed.
3. **Approval and Deployment to Production**: Once changes pass all tests, they are automatically or manually approved for deployment to the production environment.
4. **Monitoring and Rollbacks**: After deployment, monitoring tools track the application's health. If any issues arise,

automated rollback procedures restore the previous stable version.

In industries like eCommerce, financial services, and healthcare, CI/CD pipelines ensure that updates are deployed quickly and safely, minimizing downtime and improving customer experience.

Chapter 13: Performance Optimization and Scaling Your App

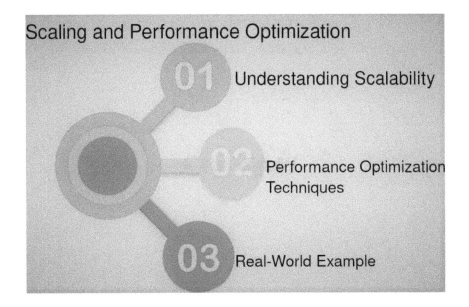

Performance Bottlenecks in Full-Stack Applications

What is Performance Optimization?

Performance optimization refers to improving the efficiency of an application, ensuring it runs as quickly and smoothly as possible. In the context of full-stack applications, performance optimization focuses on reducing load times, minimizing resource consumption, and improving the overall user experience, especially under high traffic or heavy workloads.

Performance bottlenecks are areas in the application that cause delays or slow down the entire system. These bottlenecks can be in the frontend (user interface), backend (server-side logic), or the connection between the two. Identifying and solving performance issues can help create a faster, more responsive application that can scale as your user base grows.

Common Performance Bottlenecks in Full-Stack Applications

1. **Frontend Bottlenecks (React):**
   - Slow rendering of components due to inefficient state management.
   - Unnecessary re-renders of components.
   - Large JavaScript bundles causing slow page load times.
   - Slow or blocking network requests, such as waiting for API responses.

2. **Backend Bottlenecks (Node.js and Express):**
   - Slow API responses caused by unoptimized database queries.
   - Blocking operations in Node.js, which can be caused by synchronous code or long-running tasks.
   - Lack of caching for frequently requested data.

- o Limited server resources that cannot handle high numbers of concurrent requests.

3. **Database Bottlenecks:**
   - o Slow database queries due to missing indexes, unoptimized queries, or inefficient joins.
   - o High load on the database server, especially when scaling horizontally or handling large datasets.

4. **Network Bottlenecks:**
   - o Large payloads in API responses that take longer to transfer.
   - o Latency issues when communicating between frontend and backend or between microservices.

In this chapter, we will focus on identifying and solving performance issues in both the frontend (React) and backend (Node.js/Express) of a full-stack application.

Optimizing React Performance

React is one of the most popular frameworks for building modern web applications. While React offers a declarative, component-based architecture that simplifies development, inefficient React apps can still suffer from performance bottlenecks. Fortunately,

React provides various tools and techniques to optimize performance.

Common Performance Issues in React

1. **Unnecessary Re-renders**: React components re-render every time the state or props change. If this happens too often or involves large components, it can lead to performance issues.
2. **Large JavaScript Bundles**: If the bundle size is too large, it can delay page load times, which is particularly problematic on slower networks.
3. **Inefficient Component Design**: Poorly structured components that handle too much logic or data at once can slow down rendering times.
4. **Blocking Network Requests**: Slow API calls or network latency can make the app feel unresponsive.

Techniques for Optimizing React Performance

1. **Lazy Loading**: Lazy loading allows you to load parts of your application only when they are needed, rather than loading everything at once. React supports lazy loading through the `React.lazy()` function and `Suspense` component. This is particularly useful for large apps where not all components are needed immediately.

Example of lazy loading a component:

tsx

```tsx
import React, { Suspense } from 'react';

const LazyLoadedComponent = React.lazy(() =>
import('./LazyLoadedComponent'));

const App: React.FC = () => (
  <div>
    <h1>Welcome to the App</h1>
    <Suspense fallback={<div>Loading...</div>}>
      <LazyLoadedComponent />
    </Suspense>
  </div>
);
```

Here, the `LazyLoadedComponent` will only be loaded when it's needed, improving initial load time.

2. **Memoization with `React.memo()`**: React's `memo()` function is a higher-order component that prevents unnecessary re-renders of functional components by memoizing the result. This is especially useful for components that depend on props but don't change often.

Example:

```tsx
const MyComponent: React.FC<{ value: number }>
= React.memo(({ value }) => {
  return <div>{value}</div>;
});
```

This component will only re-render if the `value` prop changes, reducing unnecessary renders.

3. **Code Splitting**: Code splitting involves splitting your application into smaller chunks, allowing the browser to download only the code that's needed for the current view. Tools like **Webpack** and **React.lazy** help in achieving code splitting.

   For example, with React's `React.lazy()` and `Suspense`, you can dynamically import only the necessary components, reducing the initial JavaScript payload.

4. **Use of `useMemo` and `useCallback` Hooks**:
   - `useMemo` is used to memoize values, preventing unnecessary recalculations.
   - `useCallback` is used to memoize functions, preventing unnecessary re-creations of the functions on each render.

Example:

tsx

```
const memoizedValue = useMemo(() =>
computeExpensiveValue(a, b), [a, b]);
const memoizedCallback = useCallback(() => {
doSomething(a, b); }, [a, b]);
```

These hooks optimize performance by ensuring expensive calculations or functions are only re-executed when their dependencies change.

5. **Virtualization**: For long lists of data (such as a table or a list of items), rendering all the elements at once can cause performance issues. **Virtualization** is a technique where only the visible items are rendered, improving both performance and memory usage.

   Libraries like **React Window** or **React Virtualized** are commonly used for this purpose.

Optimizing Node.js and Express Performance

Node.js is well-known for its high concurrency and non-blocking I/O model. However, there are still several ways to optimize Node.js and

Express applications to handle more requests and reduce server load.

Common Performance Issues in Node.js

1. **Blocking Code**: In Node.js, blocking code can severely impact performance by preventing the event loop from processing other requests. Synchronous functions or long-running tasks can cause delays in handling incoming requests.

2. **Inefficient Database Queries**: Slow database queries, especially those involving large datasets or inefficient joins, can create bottlenecks that slow down your application.

3. **Memory Leaks**: Memory leaks can accumulate over time, leading to performance degradation or even crashes.

4. **High Latency**: Slow network connections or delays in calling external APIs can affect the performance of your application.

Strategies for Optimizing Node.js and Express

1. **Asynchronous Code**: The most important aspect of Node.js is its **non-blocking, asynchronous I/O**. Always use asynchronous functions (e.g., `fs.readFile` instead of `fs.readFileSync`, or `Promise`-based database queries) to ensure that the event loop can continue processing requests while waiting for I/O operations.

2. **Cluster Mode**: Node.js is single-threaded by default, meaning it can only handle one request at a time per instance. To utilize multiple CPU cores, you can use **Node.js cluster mode** to spawn multiple processes and balance the load between them. This can significantly improve the scalability of your application.

Example using the `cluster` module:

javascript

```javascript
const cluster = require('cluster');
const http = require('http');
const numCPUs = require('os').cpus().length;

if (cluster.isMaster) {
  for (let i = 0; i < numCPUs; i++) {
    cluster.fork();
  }

  cluster.on('exit', (worker, code, signal) =>
{
    console.log(`Worker ${worker.process.pid}
died`);
  });
} else {
  http.createServer((req, res) => {
    res.writeHead(200);
```

```
      res.end('Hello World\n');
    }).listen(8000);
  }
```

This will spawn worker processes and distribute incoming requests across multiple CPU cores.

3. **Caching**: Caching frequently requested data in memory can reduce the load on your database and improve response times. Use in-memory caches like **Redis** or **Memcached** to store and retrieve data quickly.

   Example with Redis:

   javascript

```
const redis = require('redis');
const client = redis.createClient();

app.get('/data', (req, res) => {
  client.get('someKey', (err, reply) => {
    if (reply) {
      res.send(reply);
    } else {
      // Fetch data from database
      const data = fetchDataFromDatabase();
      client.setex('someKey', 3600, data); //
Cache for 1 hour
      res.send(data);
```

```
        }
      });
   });
```

4. **Load Balancing**: Load balancing helps distribute incoming traffic evenly across multiple instances of your application. Using **NGINX** or **HAProxy** can ensure that no single instance becomes overwhelmed with too many requests.

Hands-On Project: Implement Performance Improvements in Your App

In this project, we will implement performance improvements in a full-stack application (Node.js backend and React frontend). You will apply the techniques we've covered to optimize the app and handle more requests efficiently.

Step 1: Optimize React Frontend

1. **Lazy Load Components**: Implement lazy loading in your React app to reduce the initial load time.
2. **Memoization**: Use `React.memo()`, `useMemo()`, and `useCallback()` to prevent unnecessary re-renders of components.

Step 2: Optimize Node.js Backend

1. **Use Asynchronous Code**: Refactor any blocking code to use asynchronous functions or Promises.
2. **Implement Caching**: Use Redis or an in-memory cache to cache frequently requested data and reduce database load.
3. **Use Cluster Mode**: Enable clustering to take advantage of multiple CPU cores and handle more requests concurrently.

Real-World Application: How Netflix Optimizes Streaming Performance Globally

Netflix is a prime example of an application that needs to optimize performance for a global user base. Here's how Netflix tackles performance challenges:

1. **Global Content Delivery Network (CDN)**: Netflix uses a CDN to store and deliver its video content to users worldwide. This reduces latency by serving content from a location that is geographically closer to the user.
2. **Adaptive Streaming**: Netflix uses adaptive streaming to adjust the video quality based on the user's internet connection. This ensures smooth playback without buffering, even on slower networks.

3. **Microservices Architecture**: Netflix uses microservices to break down its platform into smaller, independent services. This allows them to scale each service independently based on demand and optimize resources efficiently.

4. **Real-Time Monitoring**: Netflix continuously monitors the performance of its services and adjusts resources dynamically based on usage patterns. This ensures that the service remains responsive even during peak times.

5. **Load Balancing and Caching**: Netflix employs load balancing to distribute traffic across multiple servers and caching to reduce the load on backend services.

Chapter 14: Maintaining Your Full-Stack Application

The Importance of App Maintenance

Why Maintaining Your Full-Stack App is Crucial for Longevity

Building and deploying a full-stack application is only the beginning of a successful project. **Maintenance** is a critical ongoing process that ensures your app remains functional, secure, and relevant as it grows. Regular maintenance not only keeps the application running smoothly but also prepares it for future enhancements, bug fixes, and performance improvements.

Maintenance involves the following aspects:

1. **Bug Fixes**: Addressing issues that arise in the system after the app has been deployed. Bugs can emerge due to changes in the environment, user actions, or edge cases that were not initially considered.
2. **Security Updates**: With cyber threats continuously evolving, it is important to stay on top of security vulnerabilities. Regular security patches protect the app from breaches.

3. **Feature Updates**: As user needs evolve, your app must be updated with new features to keep it competitive and valuable.

4. **Performance Enhancements**: Over time, as the user base grows and the app becomes more complex, performance might degrade. Maintenance helps address scalability and efficiency.

5. **Technology Upgrades**: As new tools and libraries are released, it is important to keep your app's technology stack up-to-date to take advantage of improvements and new features.

6. **Compliance and Regulations**: For industries like finance, healthcare, and e-commerce, maintaining compliance with industry regulations is vital for continued operations.

Why is it so important?

- **Longevity**: Without regular maintenance, applications can become outdated, slow, or prone to crashes. A well-maintained app lasts longer and remains reliable.

- **User Satisfaction**: Users expect consistent performance and new features. Regular updates demonstrate a commitment to quality, helping retain users and attract new ones.

- **Business Continuity**: Bugs, security vulnerabilities, or performance issues can impact your business operations. Maintaining your app ensures that you avoid disruptions and remain operational.

Versioning APIs and Backward Compatibility

What is API Versioning?

In the world of **full-stack applications**, APIs play a crucial role in facilitating communication between the frontend and backend. Over time, as you add new features or make changes to the app, your API will likely need to evolve. **API versioning** is a strategy used to manage these changes and ensure that existing clients aren't broken by new changes in the API.

When you make changes to your API, you want to make sure that old versions still work as expected, so users relying on the old version are not affected. This is where **backward compatibility** comes into play. API versioning helps you introduce new features, fix bugs, or improve performance without disrupting existing users.

Types of API Versioning

1. **URI Versioning**: The version number is included in the URL path. This is one of the most commonly used methods.

   Example:

   ```http
   ```

   ```
   https://api.example.com/v1/products
   https://api.example.com/v2/products
   ```

2. **Query Parameter Versioning**: The version number is passed as a query parameter in the request URL.

   Example:

   ```http
   ```

   ```
   https://api.example.com/products?version=1
   ```

3. **Header Versioning**: The version number is specified in the request headers. This keeps the URL clean and is preferred by some developers.

   Example:

   ```http
   ```

```
GET /products HTTP/1.1
Host: api.example.com
API-Version: v1
```

4. **Accept Header Versioning**: A more sophisticated approach where the version is specified in the `Accept` header.

   Example:

   ```
   http
   ```

   ```
   GET /products HTTP/1.1
   Accept: application/vnd.example.v1+json
   ```

Each versioning strategy has its pros and cons, but **URI versioning** is the most widely used for its simplicity and clarity. It ensures that users can access different versions of the API independently, preventing the new version from affecting the old one.

Handling Backward Compatibility

Ensuring backward compatibility means that any new API changes must not break the existing functionality for older clients. There are several strategies to maintain backward compatibility:

1. **Deprecation Notices**: If you plan to remove or change an API endpoint, give users advance notice by marking the endpoint

as deprecated and providing them with instructions on how to migrate to the new version.

2. **Non-Breaking Changes**: When introducing new features, ensure they do not break the existing functionality. This could include adding new optional parameters rather than changing existing required ones.

3. **Versioned Data Models**: If the data structure changes (e.g., changing the fields of a response object), ensure that the old API version returns the data in the old format while the new version supports the updated model.

4. **Clear Documentation**: Provide clear and detailed documentation on how the API changes affect users. Specify the versioning approach, highlight deprecated features, and guide users on how to transition to newer versions.

Handling Bugs and Issues Post-Deployment

Tools for Monitoring and Handling Bugs After Deployment

Once your app is deployed, bugs and issues are inevitable. Having the right tools in place can help you identify, track, and resolve these issues quickly.

1. **Error Tracking Tools:**

- o **Sentry**: A real-time error tracking tool that helps developers monitor and fix crashes in their apps. It provides detailed context for errors and helps you understand the stack trace.
- o **Rollbar**: Similar to Sentry, Rollbar helps monitor your app's errors and provides actionable insights into fixing bugs.

2. **Application Performance Monitoring (APM)**:
   - o **New Relic**: A comprehensive performance monitoring tool that tracks the performance of your app in real-time. It helps identify performance bottlenecks and provides detailed insights into the backend and frontend of your application.
   - o **Datadog**: Another powerful APM tool that helps track application performance, including monitoring databases, services, and network latency.

3. **Logging and Debugging**:
   - o **Winston**: A logging library for Node.js that allows you to create custom logging solutions. It supports logging to files, databases, or external services.
   - o **Loggly**: A cloud-based log management tool that centralizes logs from your applications and provides real-time analysis and monitoring.

4. **Crash Reporting**:

o **Firebase Crashlytics**: For mobile apps, Firebase Crashlytics helps track crashes and provides detailed reports on the cause, allowing developers to prioritize fixes.

Debugging After Deployment

1. **Reproduce the Issue Locally**: If a bug is reported in production, try to reproduce it in your local environment. Use tools like **Postman** or **Insomnia** to test the APIs with the same inputs that caused the issue.

2. **Stack Traces and Logs**: Use error tracking tools like Sentry or Loggly to capture detailed logs, including stack traces, HTTP request data, and user actions leading up to the error.

3. **Database Audits**: If the issue seems related to data corruption or a database issue, perform a database audit to check for inconsistencies.

4. **Automated Tests**: After fixing bugs, write automated tests (unit tests, integration tests) to ensure the bug is resolved and prevent regressions in the future.

Proactive Bug Prevention

- **Automated Testing**: Before deploying changes, run your unit, integration, and end-to-end tests to catch potential issues early.

- **Code Reviews**: Implement a code review process to catch bugs before they make it to production.
- **Static Code Analysis**: Use tools like **ESLint** and **Prettier** to catch code style and syntax issues before they cause bugs.

Hands-On Project: Update Your API with New Features Without Breaking Old Ones

In this hands-on project, we will update an existing API with new features while maintaining backward compatibility for existing users.

Step 1: Version Your API

Let's assume you have an API that handles user profiles. To add new features without breaking the old functionality, you need to version your API.

1. **Add a version number to your API endpoints**:

```pgsql
/api/v1/users (current version)
/api/v2/users (new version with added features)
```

2. **Update your routes** to handle different versions:

```typescript
app.get('/api/v1/users', getUsersV1);
app.get('/api/v2/users', getUsersV2);
```

3. **Write migration documentation** for users to transition from version 1 to version 2.

Step 2: Implement Backward-Compatible Changes

For example, if you're adding a new field to the user profile (e.g., `birthdate`), ensure that the new version handles it, but the old version should still function without this field.

Step 3: Update Database Models

If the data structure is changing, ensure that older versions of the API still return data in the old format. Here's how you can add a new field to the database without affecting existing users:

```typescript
const userSchemaV1 = new mongoose.Schema({
  name: String,
  email: String,
});

const userSchemaV2 = new mongoose.Schema({
```

```
name: String,
email: String,
birthdate: Date, // New field for version 2
});
```

Step 4: Testing the Updates

Use **Jest** or another testing framework to write tests that validate the new version's behavior while ensuring the old version still works. For example, you can write unit tests to verify that the old and new API versions return the correct responses.

Real-World Application: How App Updates and Patches are Handled in Banking Applications

In **banking applications**, maintaining system integrity and security is critical. These applications are subject to strict regulations and have a large user base that depends on constant uptime and security. Here's how banking apps typically handle updates and patches:

1. **Versioning of APIs**: Banking apps must maintain backward compatibility when releasing new features. For example, a bank might introduce a new **security feature** or **transaction type** without breaking existing transaction functionalities.

2. **Compliance**: Updates must ensure the application complies with industry standards such as **PCI-DSS** for payment security and **GDPR** for data privacy. Regular patches are deployed to address vulnerabilities and ensure compliance.

3. **Tested and Phased Rollouts**: Updates are first deployed to a staging environment where they are rigorously tested, including security audits. After successful testing, the updates are rolled out to a small set of users (canary deployment) before being made available to the entire user base.

4. **Real-Time Monitoring**: Banks implement real-time monitoring using tools like **Datadog**, **New Relic**, or **Prometheus** to ensure their systems remain operational. If an issue is detected, it is immediately flagged, and remediation efforts are initiated.

5. **Security Patches**: Financial institutions release **security patches** as soon as vulnerabilities are detected. These patches are often rolled out in off-peak hours to minimize disruption.

6. **User Notifications**: Users are notified of important changes, such as new features or security updates, through in-app messages, emails, or text alerts.

Chapter 15: Best Practices and Next Steps

Full-Stack JavaScript Best Practices

Building a full-stack JavaScript application requires a combination of frontend and backend skills. Whether you're working with React, Node.js, Express, or any other technology in the full-stack ecosystem, following best practices ensures your codebase is clean, maintainable, and scalable. Here are key best practices for coding, deployment, and team collaboration in full-stack JavaScript development.

1. Writing Clean and Maintainable Code

Clean code is easy to read, understand, and extend. Following clean code principles helps prevent bugs, improves collaboration, and makes future updates easier. Key strategies include:

- **Use Descriptive Variable and Function Names**: Avoid vague names like `temp` or `data`. Instead, opt for descriptive names that convey the purpose of the variable or function.

  Example:

```javascript

// Bad
let temp = 100;

// Good
let temperatureInCelsius = 100;
```

- **Keep Functions Small**: Functions should do one thing and do it well. A function that is too large is hard to understand and debug.
- **Use Comments Wisely**: While code should mostly be self-explanatory, comments can help clarify complex logic. Avoid over-commenting or explaining what is obvious from the code itself.
- **Follow Consistent Code Style**: Use a consistent style guide for indentation, spacing, and other code formatting. Tools like **Prettier** and **ESLint** can automate this and enforce rules.
- **Modularize Your Code**: Break down your application into small, reusable modules. In Node.js, create separate files for different parts of the backend logic. In React, create components that can be reused across your app.

2. Using Modern JavaScript Features

ES6+ introduces many features that improve code readability and reduce boilerplate code. These include:

- **Arrow Functions**: They make functions more concise and preserve the value of `this`.

  Example:

  javascript

  ```javascript
  // Traditional function
  function add(a, b) {
    return a + b;
  }

  // Arrow function
  const add = (a, b) => a + b;
  ```

- **Destructuring**: Simplifies the extraction of data from objects or arrays.

  Example:

  javascript

  ```javascript
  const user = { name: 'John', age: 30 };
  const { name, age } = user;
  ```

- **Async/Await**: Makes asynchronous code easier to write and read by avoiding callback hell and improving error handling.

  Example:

```javascript
async function fetchData() {
  try {
    const response = await
fetch('https://api.example.com/data');
    const data = await response.json();
    return data;
  } catch (error) {
    console.error(error);
  }
}
```

3. API Design and Versioning

Designing an API that is easy to use and extend is crucial in a full-stack application. Here are some best practices:

- **RESTful Design**: Ensure your API follows RESTful principles, where endpoints represent resources (e.g., `/users`, `/products`), and actions are performed using HTTP verbs (GET, POST, PUT, DELETE).
- **Versioning**: As your API evolves, version it to avoid breaking existing clients. Use clear versioning in your URLs (e.g., `/api/v1/users`).
- **Error Handling**: Provide meaningful error messages with status codes, making it easy for users to diagnose issues (e.g., `400 Bad Request`, `404 Not Found`).

4. Security Best Practices

Security is essential in modern web development. Follow these best practices to secure your full-stack application:

- **Secure Passwords**: Always hash passwords before storing them. Use libraries like **bcrypt** for hashing and salting passwords.

  Example:

  ```javascript
  const bcrypt = require('bcryptjs');
  const hashedPassword = await bcrypt.hash(password, 10);
  ```

- **JWT Authentication**: Use **JSON Web Tokens (JWT)** for stateless authentication. Ensure that tokens are securely signed and stored (e.g., in HTTP-only cookies).
- **Input Validation**: Validate user input both on the frontend and backend to prevent SQL injection, XSS, and other attacks. Use libraries like **Joi** or **express-validator** to simplify validation.
- **Rate Limiting**: Protect your application from brute force attacks by limiting the number of requests a user can make

in a given time period. Use middleware like **express-rate-limit.**

Scaling Your Full-Stack App

When your application starts gaining traction, it needs to be able to handle large numbers of users and vast amounts of data. Scaling involves ensuring that your application can continue to perform well as usage increases. Here are strategies to scale your full-stack JavaScript app effectively.

1. Load Balancing

A single instance of your application may not be able to handle all the traffic. **Load balancing** helps distribute incoming traffic across multiple server instances, ensuring that no single server becomes overwhelmed. Popular load balancers include:

- **NGINX**: A reverse proxy server that distributes traffic between multiple application servers.
- **HAProxy**: A high-performance TCP/HTTP load balancer that can manage large-scale systems.
- **Cloud Load Balancers**: If you are using cloud services like AWS, Google Cloud, or Azure, they often provide built-in load balancing tools.

2. Horizontal Scaling

Horizontal scaling involves adding more instances of your application to distribute the load. This is more cost-effective and scalable than **vertical scaling**, which involves adding more resources (CPU, memory) to a single instance.

- **Docker Containers**: Use **Docker** to containerize your application and deploy it across multiple machines.
- **Kubernetes**: Kubernetes is an open-source container orchestration platform that automates the deployment, scaling, and management of containerized applications.

3. Caching

Caching is a crucial technique for scaling. By caching frequently accessed data, you can reduce the load on your database and speed up response times.

- **Database Caching**: Use **Redis** or **Memcached** to cache database query results and reduce the number of database hits.
- **API Caching**: Cache API responses using HTTP caching headers or services like **Cloudflare** to improve performance and reduce latency.

4. Database Sharding and Replication

As your database grows, it may become necessary to partition it across multiple machines to handle large amounts of data. This is known as **sharding**. In addition, **replication** can be used to distribute the read load by creating multiple copies of your database.

- **Sharding**: Split your database into smaller, more manageable pieces (shards), each hosted on a different server.
- **Replication**: Use replication to create copies of your database to handle more read requests. This can also help with disaster recovery.

5. Asynchronous Processing

Handling requests asynchronously can help offload time-consuming tasks (like sending emails or processing payments) from the main request-response cycle. Tools like **RabbitMQ**, **Kafka**, or **Bull** (a Node.js task queue) can be used to implement background processing.

- **Queueing Systems**: Use a queue to store tasks and process them in the background, allowing your app to remain responsive even during high loads.

Exploring Other Technologies for Full-Stack Development

As full-stack JavaScript development evolves, new technologies and approaches continue to emerge. Here are some popular alternatives and complementary tools that can take your app to the next level.

1. GraphQL

GraphQL is an alternative to REST APIs, allowing clients to request exactly the data they need and nothing more. This reduces over-fetching and under-fetching of data and improves performance, especially on mobile devices with limited bandwidth.

- **Benefits:**
    - **Flexible Queries**: Clients can request only the data they need.
    - **Single Endpoint**: Unlike REST, which typically has multiple endpoints, GraphQL exposes a single endpoint for all requests.
    - **Strong Typing**: GraphQL schemas define the structure of the API, making it easier to work with and maintain.

2. Serverless Functions

Serverless architecture allows you to run backend code without worrying about server management. With serverless platforms like **AWS Lambda**, **Azure Functions**, or **Google Cloud Functions**, you can deploy small pieces of logic that run in response to events (e.g., HTTP requests, database changes).

- **Benefits**:
    - **Scalability**: Automatically scales based on the number of incoming requests.
    - **Cost-Effective**: You only pay for the compute time used, rather than for always-on servers.
    - **Focus on Code**: Developers can focus on writing business logic without worrying about infrastructure.

3. Cloud Services

Cloud platforms like **AWS**, **Google Cloud**, and **Microsoft Azure** provide various services to help scale, monitor, and manage your full-stack applications. These services include compute power, storage, databases, caching, load balancing, and machine learning capabilities.

- **Elastic Scaling**: Automatically scale resources (e.g., compute instances, databases) based on demand.

- **Managed Services**: Use fully managed services like **Amazon RDS** or **Google Cloud Firestore** for databases, reducing the operational overhead.

Hands-On Project: Apply the Best Practices to Refactor and Scale Your Full-Stack App

In this hands-on project, you will apply the best practices discussed in this chapter to refactor and scale your full-stack application.

Step 1: Refactor the Codebase

- **Apply Clean Code Principles**: Refactor the code to ensure it follows best practices for readability, maintainability, and efficiency.
- **Use Modern JavaScript Features**: Replace older JavaScript code with ES6+ features like arrow functions, destructuring, and async/await.

Step 2: Optimize the Application

- **Implement Lazy Loading in React**: Use `React.lazy()` and `Suspense` to reduce the initial load time.
- **Optimize Node.js Performance**: Implement clustering, caching, and asynchronous code to handle more requests.

Step 3: Scale the Application

- **Set Up Load Balancing**: Use **NGINX** or **HAProxy** to distribute traffic across multiple instances of your Node.js app.
- **Implement Horizontal Scaling**: Use Docker and Kubernetes to scale your app across multiple servers.

Step 4: Deploy to the Cloud

- **Deploy to AWS**: Set up your application on AWS using EC2 instances, RDS for your database, and Elastic Load Balancer for distributing traffic.
- **Automate Deployment**: Set up a CI/CD pipeline using **GitHub Actions** or **Jenkins** for automated deployment.

Next Steps: Resources for Further Learning and Taking Your Skills to the Next Level

To continue growing as a full-stack developer, here are some next steps and resources:

1. Advanced React Concepts

- Learn about **React Context API** for global state management.

- Dive into **React Hooks** (e.g., `useReducer`, `useEffect`) to manage more complex state logic.

2. Master Backend Development

- Deepen your understanding of **Node.js** by exploring frameworks like **NestJS** and **Fastify**.
- Learn about **microservices** and **GraphQL** as alternatives to RESTful APIs.

3. Explore Cloud Development

- Dive deeper into cloud platforms like AWS, Google Cloud, or Azure, and learn about deploying serverless applications using **AWS Lambda** or **Google Cloud Functions**.

4. Contribute to Open Source

- Contribute to open-source projects on GitHub to gain experience with large codebases and collaborate with other developers.

5. Keep Up with Industry Trends

- Stay updated on the latest trends in full-stack development by following blogs, podcasts, and industry conferences.

www.ingramcontent.com/pod-product-compliance
Lightning Source LLC
LaVergne TN
LVHW022341060326
832902LV00022B/4175